HEART GUARDS

HOW TO PROTECT YOUR HEART OF WORSHIP IN A CORRUPT SOCIETY

BRANNON CARNES

Copyright © 2025 Brannon Carnes
First Paperback and Hardback Edition

All rights reserved. No part of this publication may be reproduced, distributed, or transmitted in any form or by any means, including photocopying, recording, or other electronic or mechanical methods, without the prior written permission of the publisher, except in thecase of brief quotations embodied in critical reviews andcertain other noncommercial uses permitted by copyright law.
For permission requests, write to the publisher, addressed "Attention: Permissions Coordinator," at the address below.

Some names, businesses, places, events, locales, incidents, and identifying details inside this book have been changed to protect the privacy of individuals.

Published by Freiling Agency, LLC.

P.O. Box 1264
Warrenton, VA 20188

www.FreilingAgency.com

PB ISBN: 978-1-963701-85-2
HB ISBN: 978-1-969826-01-6
E-book ISBN: 978-1-969826-00-9

For information, please write:

Brannon Carnes Ministries International
P.O. Box 573
Bloomingdale, IL 60108

Visit us online at
www.brannoncarnesministries.com

Bible versions used:

New Living Translation (NLT)

Holy Bible, New Living Translation, copyright © 1996, 2004, 2015 by Tyndale House Foundation. Used by permission of Tyndale House Publishers, Inc., Carol Stream, Illinois 60188. All rights reserved.

The Message (MSG)

Copyright © 1993, 2002, 2018 by Eugene H. Peterson.

New King James Version (NKJV)

The New King James Version®. Copyright © 1982 by Thomas Nelson. Used by permission. All rights reserved.

King James Version (KJV)

Public Domain

The Passion Translation

Scripture quotations marked TPT are from The Passion Translation®. Copyright © 2017, 2018, 2020 by Passion & Fire Ministries, Inc. Used by permission. All rights reserved. ThePassionTranslation.com.

Amplified Bible, Classic Edition (AMPC)

Copyright © 1954, 1958, 1962, 1964, 1965, 1987 by The Lockman Foundation.

DEDICATION

First, to the One on Whom I lavish my worship, Jesus Christ! He alone is my Savior and Lord. Second, to the wife of my youth, Denise! You are the love of my life, the wind in my sails, and the inspiration for writing this book. You are indeed one of the greatest examples of true, heartfelt worship.

CONTENTS

Introduction: The Heart of the Matter xi
Acknowledgments ix

The Foundation

1. My Story 5
2. Heart Condition 13
3. Soaking 25
4. Heart Diagnosis 39

The Application

5. Heart Guards 51
6. Personal Prayer Altar 75
7. Put Your Heart Into It 83

References 93
About the Author 95

ACKNOWLEDGMENTS

To my musical parents, Tim and Monica Amstutz. You are responsible for laying and securing the foundations of praise and worship in me. I am forever grateful to the Lord for you!

To the late Dr. Carlton R. Arthurs. As the apostle Paul mentions in 1 Corinthians 4:15, "For though you have ten thousand instructors in Christ, yet you do not have many fathers..." He stepped in when I desperately needed fathering to catapult me into marriage, family, and ministry. I am forever grateful.

To Pastor James E. Ward, Jr. You are more than a pastor and a friend. You are my covenant brother. Your life has modeled a man whose heart of worship is well protected in a corrupt society. You inspire me to live this out each day. Thank you, sir.

To the BCMI Board Members & Partners. Thank you for ten years of helping nations connect with God. You are partakers in every victory of this ministry!

To the Insight Church tribe. Thanks for the honor of serving you, watching over your souls. It's a privilege doing life together with you!

To Mr. Tom Freiling and the entire team at Freiling Agency. From the beginning of our working relationship I have sensed the effortless chemistry and rich comradery we share. What an amazing experience to create literary history with world-class people! Thank you.

INTRODUCTION

THE HEART OF THE MATTER

The year 2020 has changed the landscape of the world. During the pandemic, we are introduced to phrases like "shelter-in-place" and "social distancing." We are presented with a new way of existing, a new social reality. Everyone 25 years old and older mildly compares this to the transformation of 9-11.

We find ourselves forced to change our way of life, scale down our operations, and return to the fundamentals of existence. Concepts like work, education, shopping, and eating out have become more challenging than ever. Things we once took for granted, namely sanitation products, paper towels, and toilet paper, are now special commodities. Essentially, the pandemic has helped us reprioritize our lives so that what matters in life has returned to the position of top priority: faith and family.

In light of returning to top priorities, we are having to revisit the way we do church. The church is no exception to change, especially as it relates to worship *in* the church. Every pastor, leader, and layperson is standing face-to-face with the stark realities of a paradigm shift. Honestly, our hearts have taken a beating when it comes to grappling with changes in our world, our nation, and our personal lives. It's easy to harden one's heart to the constant tension between experiences from within and from without. Believing what you see in the culture or what you have been taught growing up in the church. These realities can lead to a heart that is callous to the Word of God, not to mention worshipping God.

On February 20, 2021, the word of the Lord came to me saying:

I am not pleased with the worship on earth. Many of My people don't understand what it means to truly worship Me. I want pure worship on earth. I want pure worship in My church.

Well, what does God want regarding worship? Two Scriptures leave us with similar thoughts on God's position regarding true worship: Psalm 15:1-2 and Psalm 24:3-4.

Who may worship in your sanctuary, Lord? Who may enter your presence on your holy hill? Those who lead blameless lives and do what is right, speaking the truth from sincere hearts.

Who may climb the mountain of the Lord? Who may stand in His holy place? Only those whose hands and hearts are pure, who do not worship idols and never tell lies.

Both passages speak of the heart. It seems that when we deal with matters of the heart, we begin conditioning ourselves for worship. There is a connection with our hearts and worship of God.

Well, I must say that God has not changed nor has His position on how to approach Him in worship. He is indeed the same yesterday, today, and forevermore (Hebrews 13:8). The question is, "How do we lead blameless lives?" and "How do we have pure hands and hearts?"

Heart Guards™ is designed to stir that hope in you again, to awaken that longing to see God move in both private and corporate times of worship. But not just a carbon copy of the past. I believe that faith is also being stirred in you as you read this book to believe God for more than what we can ask, think, or imagine (Ephesians

3:20). It goes beyond our limited references of past awakenings and revivals. I believe God is saying to us, "Remove every limitation of the past as you read this book so that I can blow your mind, your imagination, and your references out of the water!" God is big enough to merge our past with our present and future, all in one moment! He's preparing us for a worship revolution!

In *Heart Guards*™, you will receive both the inspiration to move you towards personal and corporate breakthroughs, and the practical tools to help develop and encourage your worship teams, worship leaders, as well as any disciple of Christ to regain connection with God. "Where are we going?" you may ask. We're going back to the foundations: The conditioning of our hearts for lifestyles of worship to God.

Heart Guards™ is not focused on shifting the blame or promoting victimization. We have plenty of that in our world. The goal of *Heart Guards*™ is to:

1. Diagnose Our Hearts
2. Condition Our Hearts
3. Protect Our Hearts

In doing so, we will realign our hearts and press the reset button of worship that prepares and preserves us for the second coming of Christ. I truly believe that the genuine desire of many people of faith is to draw the presence of God into their personal and corporate worship experiences. I believe many Christians want to see heartfelt worship emerge in the local church again, resulting in the demonstrations of the Holy Spirit as we read about in Scripture: blind eyes opened, deaf ears unstopped, yokes destroyed, and burdens removed, people turning from the power of Satan to God (see Acts 26:18). I believe these are the results of the worship services of the past.

Wouldn't it be nice if the goal of every worship team/leader is to leave a service so that the congregation doesn't remember them, but remembers their encounter with God? I often say that it would be great to walk off the stage, and no one knows that we've left the stage because they are so taken by the King! What if the success of a worship service is gauged by notable miracles, heartfelt expressions of repentance, and/or the gentle whispers of clear direction from the voice of God? What if we are so focused on the King that we are no longer focused on the time? What if we left the service and sensed that God was saying, "I've been worshipped today!"? I believe this is possible, but it starts in our hearts, the conditioning of our hearts.

Scripture says, "…the love of many will grow cold" (see Matt. 24:12). We're seeing the beginnings of that today. People are getting out of love and they are letting it be made known on social media. But we want to genuinely receive God's love and grow in love.

The two overarching mandates of *Heart Guards*™ are:

A. To "Set up road signs; put up guideposts. Mark well the path by which you came…" Jeremiah 31:21 (NLT). Unearth the ancient pathways that lead straight to the heart of God.

B. To prepare hearts for the end-times. James 5:8 says, "You also be patient. Establish your hearts, for the coming of the Lord is at hand."

Before you read this book, please pray this prayer based upon Ephesians 1:17-19:

Heavenly Father, the God of our Lord Jesus Christ, the Father of glory, give to me the spirit of wisdom and revelation in the knowledge of You, so that the eyes of my understanding are enlightened; that I may know what is the hope of Your calling, what are the riches of the glory of Your inheritance in the saints, and what is the exceeding greatness of Your power toward me, a believer, according to the working of Your mighty power. In Jesus' name. Amen!

Now…it's time to establish your heart!

THE FOUNDATIONS

Set up signposts to mark your trip home. Get a good map. Study the road conditions. The road out is the road back. Come back, dear virgin Israel, come back to your hometowns (Jeremiah 31:21, MSG).

1

MY STORY

To start our journey, I have to take you back to the humble beginnings in the cornfields of the Midwest, to my hometown, Michigan City, Indiana. With a corner of Lake Michigan as its claim to fame (and the quickest way to locate it on a map), Michigan City boasts of its white sandy beach, quaint lighthouse, vast outlet mall, and small-town façade. Personally, it represents a season of small beginnings, of which I am unashamed. The memories are picture-perfect in my mind. Deeply etched in the recesses of my thoughts are the modest people in a simple town giving way to a humble narrative. These are the memories that push me forward, yet keep me grounded in core values.

My dad, the late Edward E. Carnes, was my first exposure to a musician, a worship leader, and, more importantly, a man of God. The Lord gave me a father who was perfect for me, instilling into his children the disciplines that govern a respectable life. My dad was an example of what hard work looks like. His military background was the backdrop of the training which led to our becoming contributors to society.

Furthermore, we were fortunate to have a mother, the late Shirley L. Carnes, who has demonstrated the love of God, the essence of nurturing and encouraging. She was the first gracious woman in my life and the standard of what a life cheerleader should be like. Was I spoiled? If 'spoiled' is being filled with so much encouragement every day that it could last five decades later, recalling one-liners and scenarios verbatim…then yes…I confess I was unashamedly spoiled!

However, this isn't just about a small-town, African-American family dynamic. This is the story of a simple boy destined for global travels and an international platform made specifically for worship ministry, long before worship ministry gained its popularity.

EARLY YEARS OF MUSIC

My musical story began when I was only three years old. Yes, I recall some details as early as 1973. The moment I finished eating breakfast, I would jet into the living room of our small, three-bedroom government house. It was there my mom would help me take the records out of their sleeves and place them onto the extended-play record player. I remember sitting on our chocolate brown suede, three-seater couch listening to song after song.

I would sit and play for several minutes at a time (and when I say play, I mean act like I was playing an actual piano). I would mimic gospel music greats like Andrae' Crouch, Edwin Hawkins, and Milton Bronson and the Thompson Community Singers. There was a sound that spoke to me during my tender years. More than that, there was a pioneering spirit that was weaved into the musical fibers of my life to give me the sound that I would have 20 years later.

During my teenage years, I wasn't as social except for church events. I didn't have a lot of friends. However, I poured everything into my art and music. Although God began to deal with me at age nine, my musical abilities didn't begin to manifest until my tween years. I began playing the keyboard next to my dad. By age eleven, I could carry a service all by myself.

There were many church services and events to follow, which contributed to my early training. Summer tent services, winter revival meetings, and everything in between were woven into my musical and spiritual tapestry. I was fortunate to be exposed to a 21st-century example of the New Testament Church. We encountered deliverance, healing, tongues, and interpretation of tongues. In the eyes of man, we were insignificant. But through God's eyes, I believe my dad (the pastor) was successful. Men were being saved, people were being shepherded, and children were being raised in safe households of faith.

20th CENTURY LOOK AT THE PIONEERING SPIRIT

Whenever I'm asked about the people who influenced my musical journey, names come to mind like Andrae' Crouch, The Hawkins Family, The Winans, Michael W. Smith, Amy Grant, Commissioned, Carmen, Jessy Dixon, The Thompson Community Choir, Ron Kenoly, Graham Kendrick, Donnie McClurkin, BeBe & CeCe Winans, Tramaine Hawkins, just to name a few.

The Christian music of the '70s was the soundtrack of revival in the hearts and lives of many young people of that day. My parents were young adults who gravitated to this new sound. Our home was filled with songs like *Jesus Is the Answer, Oh Happy Day, I Wish We'd All Been Ready*, and many other songs with a full gospel message and a pioneering sound.

The small beginnings were a testament to the Lord taking the weak things of this world to confound the wise (see 1 Cor. 1:27). This place of small beginnings would later become the epicenter of a global revival and awakening that would transcend nationalities, denominations, age groups, and socioeconomic status. The Spirit of God would be poured out just like on the day of Pentecost.

The Spirit of God *is* the Pioneering Spirit. He is the One who causes ethnicities, denominations, ages, and economic diversities to come together under one roof and supernaturally love one another.

In my humble opinion, I believe that we are in another dispensation of the Pioneering Spirit. I believe with all of my heart that

God has hidden treasure on the earth. There's so much more to discover inside God's creative people. As there are millions of songs written, there are millions more that have yet to be revealed!

The soundtrack of each generation is housed in the heart of that particular generation and released during an awakening to God. God's Holy Spirit is moving us to unearth the new songs and sounds that will declare His glory on the earth.

FOUNDATIONS

There is an atmosphere that inspires and trains a pioneer. My atmosphere was a place called Oral Roberts University, a liberal arts, Pentecostal, Full Gospel university. And like my background, this university made no apologies for its embrace of the gifts of the Spirit as seen in the New Testament. From 1989-99, this was my introduction to a different style and sound. The Music Ministries Department trained and sent out worship leaders and teams on mission trips every summer. Ministry teams would go into all the world and conduct concerts and minister in both word and song in churches, schools, orphanages, prisons, parks and anywhere college students were welcomed.

When I arrived at ORU in 1989, the Music Ministry Department was under the direction of Tim and Monica Amstutz. They had laid the foundation for praise and worship long before my arrival. These foundations which have stood the test of time, were also laid in me. And I am still building upon them today.

I call Tim Amstutz the musical father of my life. He taught me how to lead worship. He taught me how to be sensitive to the moving of the Holy Spirit during a service in any type of atmosphere. He helped me understand how to gauge the audience, knowing how to sense what God is doing in a particular service. He took me under his wing and taught me about worship, anointing, and excellence. This was an investment during my beginnings.

MY STORY

This atmosphere of the pioneering spirit was also an open door to travel the world. My introduction to foreign travel was the Music Ministry mission trip to Holland in the Summer of 1990. This was the fulfillment of a prophecy I received when I was eight years old, of which my parents reminded me before leaving for my first overseas trip.

My training continued through the exposure of major pioneering worship leaders like Ron Kenoly, Don Moen, Terry Law, Kent Henry, and Darlene Zschech, who at different times would grace our university stage. We were also very fortunate to have some of them be a part of our guest faculty in our Worship Ensemble Class (where we used the worship textbook called *Exploring Worship* by Bob Sorge).

> "...Laying a worship **foundation** in me upon which I am **building** today."

It was a privilege to be at a university that embraced a new sound as well as the people who blazed new trails, even in the face of opposition.

My training was put to the test in 1993. At age 23, I was asked to co-direct the music ministry department as well as lead the 5,000 students, faculty, and staff in worship each week in chapels and Sunday night services. I was given the amazing opportunity to be a producer, songwriter, and arranger for ORU's worship album of 1996. Although this was my second album, it was the project that would catapult me into the growing genre of praise and worship music.

After leading worship for five years at ORU, my journey takes me back to Indiana to help in my dad's church. Soon after that, I receive a full-time worship-leading position at Wheaton Christian Center in Carol Stream, Illinois. This is where I connect with Pastor Carlton Arthurs, my second 'father in the faith' (my dad being the first). For the next six years, I would be groomed for the pastorate. Stepping into the new role of Worship Pastor helped me pour into others what was poured into me.

Sixteen-and-a-half years have passed and I have recently transitioned from the full-time worship leader position (at Wheaton Christian Center) to being an associate pastor at Insight Church (Pastor James E. Ward, Jr). Furthermore, I have begun embarking on a new career in teaching music and art to students ranging from ages 12 to 17.

With over 30 years of worship experience, I have been given the mandate to help the next generation discover the hidden treasures within themselves to touch the heart of God. Worship is from our hearts to God's heart, and with His help you will experience this great exchange in greater measure.

And I will give you a new heart, and I will put a new spirit in you. I will take out your stony, stubborn heart and give you a tender, responsive heart. And I will put my Spirit in you so that you will follow my decrees and be careful to obey my regulations (Ezekiel 36:26-27, NLT).

2

HEART CONDITION

As you continue reading this book, you will find that music is secondary when it comes to worship. We *do* understand that music is a tool, but other things take precedence when it comes to worshipping the Creator. And may I add that this is not steeped in a spirit of legalism, but rather built on our response to His love for us. More on that later.

We begin our journey in a place where authenticity is forged, hope is born, and faith is realized. In this place, seeds are planted and the harvest is gathered. Everything genuine comes from this place called the *heart*. Scripture calls it the innermost being, or the spirit-man, or the hidden man of the heart. No matter the terminology, there's a part of us where sincere feelings, experiences, and passions are housed that cannot always be explained or denied.

We have the responsibility of giving God complete access to our hearts. No matter the trauma, struggle, or offense, only He can recalibrate the human heart to its original purpose and affections, clearing the debris that leads to the path of pure worship to God.

When talking about our lifestyles of worship to God, we can't help but think about the condition of our hearts. We must understand that true worship comes from this deep place inside our hearts that is connected to God through a personal relationship with Jesus Christ.

Recently, my wife began to clear out her closet, getting rid of old clothes that she no longer wears. During the decluttering, someone gave her a new wardrobe. It was as if she unknowingly cleared out the old stuff in preparation for the new stuff, many with the price tags still on them.

As we clear out the old stuff in our hearts, we are preparing for the new thing God wants to do inside of us. Second Corinthians 5:17 says, "Therefore if any man be in Christ, he is a new creature; old things are passed away; behold, all things are become new."

> The **'Spring-Cleaning'** of the Heart

This is the "spring-cleaning" of the heart. "How does this happen? How do I clean out my heart?" With the assumption that we have received Jesus as Savior and Lord of our lives, we can then acknowledge that we have toxic objects within our hearts, the debris from the past lifestyle of sin. When we allow God to shine His light on these objects, it's just the beginning of the decluttering process. The Spirit of the Lord helps us navigate through the 'spring-cleaning' of our hearts while providing us with tools, like the Word of God, to take the next step in dealing with the negative things within our hearts.

Isaiah 40 opens our eyes to the realities of the depths of the human heart. By using natural examples of mountains and valleys, smooth paths, and tough terrain, Isaiah charts a safe route through the depths of the human heart. We plunge into the extreme contrast of emotions and passions that span the entire scale of human expression. Let's take a closer look at what lies within the heart of man through the eyes of the prophet Isaiah.

1. Prepare the Way of the Lord (Conditioning)
2. Valleys Exalted (Affirming)
3. Mountains and Hills Made Low (Humbling)
4. Crooked Places Straightened Out (Delivering)
5. Rough Places Smoothed Out (Regulating)
6. The Glory Revealed (Promoting)

HEART CONDITION

PREPARE THE WAY (Conditioning)

As the apostle Paul did in his epistles, I would like to use athletic analogies to bring home these timeless truths within this topic. Preparing the way begins with the conditioning process. Before a runner runs a marathon, or an athlete competes in the Olympics, they must condition their bodies to maintain strength and stamina during extreme physical exertion. The well-prepared athlete doesn't fold under competitive pressure nor give in to the psychological tension between physical strain and mental focus.

> "...**Renewing** your mind, **conditioning** you for the rough road ahead."

The conditioning process of the heart—or preparing the way of the Lord—begins with opening our hearts to God's Word and His nature. Romans 12:2 says, "And do not be conformed to this world, but be transformed by the renewing of your mind…" Preparing the way of the Lord begins with renewing your mind, conditioning you for the rough road ahead. When troubles come and the last thing you feel like doing is worshipping God, your mind has been renewed, it has been fortified to withstand the tough terrain. You now rise above feelings, circumstances, and fears. Mind renewal helps clear the path that leads to sincere worship of God.

The Word of God has a way of rewiring and rearranging our minds to think about what He wants us to think to ultimately do what He wants us to do. Philippians 4:8 says, "Fix your thoughts on what is true, and honorable, and right, and pure, and lovely, and admirable. Think about things that are excellent and worthy of praise." One thing the apostle Paul didn't say is, "Only if you feel like it." The general undertone is "discipline yourself."

We can condition our hearts through the renewing of our minds, disciplining our minds to think of good things. We have a plaque on the wall that says it best, "Focus on the Good."

VALLEYS EXALTED (Affirming)

This is the place where humility is rewarded. Those who have been forgotten are remembered and honored. If you've been serving behind the scenes, and no one has stroked your back, you will be exalted in due time. Promotion is coming!

Matthew 6:6 says, "But when you pray, go away by yourself, shut the door behind you, and pray to your Father in private. Then your Father, who sees everything, will reward you." Simply put, what you sow in seclusion, will be harvested in public. So, keep on praying behind the scenes. Keep worshipping God by yourself and see the harvest unfold in public at the appropriate time.

I think of young David in Scripture when he took care of his father's sheep. He was in seclusion. He worshipped God behind the scenes. He sang to God behind the scenes. He fought battles behind the scenes. Everything he did behind the scenes was eventually rewarded publicly.

One of David's greatest rewards was when God referred to him as a man after His own heart. Do you think God said this because of David's public life? I think not. Historically, knowing how God deals with people, I believe God called David a man after His own heart because of private devotion. He developed a trusting relationship with God while in seclusion.

It's in the valley that favor is forged between you and God. It's in the secret place that God sees you drawing close to Him, so He draws close to you (James 4:8).

MOUNTAINS AND HILLS MADE LOW (Humbling)

Pride will be pulled down. Arrogance, competition, and selfish ambition—the mountains and hills—will all be removed from the heart. They are pulled down in Jesus' name. We want our hearts conditioned for God's Word and His nature.

Every knee shall eventually bow, so let's bow ours now (see Philippians 2:10-11). Don't wait until judgment day to bow down; do it right now!

Those things we have exalted above the knowledge of God, the things we have made idols, must be pulled down. I will go as far as to say the unbiblical worldviews—thoughts and opinions that shape the culture around us—are invisible idols to be snatched down in our hearts (see 2 Corinthians 10:5). There is a worldly way of doing things and a God-honoring way of doing things and the two are opposites in the scope of eternity. Isaiah 55:8-9 explains that God's thoughts and ways are completely different from ours. Romans 8:7 says it like this,

For the sinful nature is always hostile to God. It never did obey God's laws, and it never will.

It behooves us to cast down those idols set up in our hearts that are in direct opposition to God's desires for us found in His Word.

CROOKED PLACES STRAIGHTENED OUT (Delivering)

This is where wickedness is made righteous. God will deliver those who are ensnared by deception. Anything that has veered from the straight and narrow path, must be brought back to the pathway of God.

Get rid of everything that is unrighteous. This can apply to unrighteous relationships, unhealthy music, toxic environments, etc., so get rid of it. The negative narratives shaped by the media (including social media) must be replaced with sound biblical truths.

We must reject the societal norms that are twisted and wicked at their very core. All agendas, both hidden and blatant, must be exposed and eliminated from our hearts. We cannot afford to participate in the wickedness of this world but rather expose them (see Ephesians 5:11-14).

ROUGH PLACES SMOOTHED OUT (Regulating)

Within the human heart, there is the capacity to carry decades of offenses. However, when we condition our hearts for the Word of God and His nature, we are preparing to release all offenses. We can forgive and be forgiven. God will melt the heart of stone (see Eph. 4:32; Mark 11:25).

When you stand praying or worshiping God in His presence, forgive! This is one of the most important ingredients to the conditioning of our hearts. Forgiveness is critically important to having our hearts prepared for God's ways and His nature.

THE GLORY REVEALED (Promoting)

The glory of God is not someplace in the "sweet by-and-by." God has created a space in our hearts to understand glory (see Hab. 2:14; 2 Cor. 4:6). The Glory will dominate our hearts. The heart has a massive capacity for experiences, desires, and God Himself.

Scripture gives us a brief look into the true capacity of the soul of man. Jesus encounters a demon-possessed man and asks the demon what his name is. He replied, "My name is Legion because there are many of us inside this man" (Mark 5:9). Jesus gave the evil spirits permission to leave the possessed man and enter the herd of pigs. If the evil spirits each possessed one pig, then there were at least 2,000 spirits logged inside the soul of this man, for 2,000 pigs were feeding on a nearby hillside.

Think about it: If we were so open to God and gave Him full access to our hearts, then we can embody at least 2,000 attributes of God!

THREE CHAMBERS OF THE HEART

The Word of the Lord came to me saying:

"I have placed inside of you a cathedral of praise, a chapel of adoration, and a room of worship. You access them by faith. There is no limit as to what I can do with you as you flow in and out of these dimension," says the Lord.

CATHEDRAL OF PRAISE: The Gates of Thanksgiving

This is the place for the masses. It's a large gathering, like a megachurch. This is a massive place for the worship concert in an arena. It's a place where diversity and variety of genres are celebrated. The Cathedral of Praise also happens to be the place where talent, skill set, and cultures are acknowledged. The production of the worship experience is highlighted.

Venders, professionals, theatrical productions and everything is going on here. Food courts, coffee shops, and malls are the norm in the cathedral.

CHAPEL OF ADORATION: The Courts of Praise

This is the place of unity. It's a place where everyone who gathers is in one accord; they have all things in common. We're not just talking about the numeric value. We are talking about the hearts coming into alignment, singing together, worshipping together, doing life together. Large enough to make a joyful noise, yet small enough to have your soul watched over. There's top quality (and perhaps some quantity), but there's also sincere accountability here.

All affection is on things above, a beautiful focus. Unified in doctrine, vision, and purpose. Everyone is on the same page when it comes to values. It's where metropolis meets small town. It's what the Scriptures call "the household of faith" (see Galatians 6:10).

Finally, lyrically sound doctrine and God-centered songs are acknowledged here. We sing more Word-based songs. We sing more prophetically as the Spirit of God directs. The Chapel of Adoration is the local church.

ROOM OF WORSHIP: The Holy of Holies

This is a special place in our hearts. It's a place of solitude. It is reserved for you and God, you have come here to be with Him alone. It's a place where you do business with God, a safe, secret place.

Your heart is exposed in the room of worship. This is a safe, yet uncomfortable place. Pride is stripped away, no masks (literally), no productions. You are exposed and loved and embraced at the same time. You are changed in God's presence.

Music becomes optional; it's no longer relevant. It becomes background noise. Few words are exchanged. In this place, the trust relationship is forged. Ministry is birthed. Power is invested. The fire of the Holy Spirit burns away the dross in our hearts while empowering us for effective ministry. This indeed is where character and power meet.

> "...where **character** and **power** meet."

The Holy of Holies is where the heart is conditioned for the Word of God. The Word needs good soil. The presence of God is the way we soften the hardness of our hearts, thus making it good ground for the Word of God.

As you can see, the Room of Worship is essential to the thriving life of every believer. Without this room, we might as well not even profess to be Christians. We would go through the motions with no tangible evidence that we belong to God, or that we are completely His. It's in this secret place that our lives are transformed and conditioned to live completely for God.

The eyes of the Lord search the whole earth in order to strengthen those whose hearts are fully committed to him (2 Chorn. 16:9a).

PRACTICAL GUIDE

We learned through the prophet Isaiah how to:

- Prepare our hearts
- Humble our hearts
- Reject pride
- Avoid deception
- Release Offenses
- Receive more of God's attributes

How do we begin to 'prepare the way of the Lord'?

Preparing the way of the Lord begins with renewing our minds, conditioning our minds to righteousness and not victimization. What God's Word says about us is more important than how we feel about ourselves, or on which side of the tracks we grew up.

In the three Chambers of the Heart, we learned that:

There's a place in worship to God for the masses, the local church, and your personal time. They are called the Cathedral, the Chapel, and the Room.

But his delight is in the law of the Lord, and in His law he meditates day and night. He shall be like a tree planted by rivers of water, that brings forth its fruit in its season, whose leaf also shall not wither; and whatever he does shall prosper (Psalm 1:2-3, NKJV).

3

SOAKING

There is a principle that is found in both natural and spiritual realms: it's called the law of saturation. Whatever you soak in will be the aroma you release. You are what you eat, drink, talk, think, and be around daily.

You can saturate yourself in the light of God's glory or the darkness of the enemy's lair. Whether good or bad, you will be filled with whatever you consistently take in. Scripture says,

For as he thinketh in his heart, so is he; eat and drink, saith he to thee; but his heart is not with thee (Proverbs 23:7, KJV).

Your life can be a fragrant scent of thanksgiving and praise or a horrific stench of murmuring and complaining. It all depends upon what you saturate in. Your environment, your music, or your words can be an aromatic atmosphere or a foul one. The choice is yours.

Our lives are filled with distractions. Everyone and everything has the potential to dominate our attention. Every day we are given a choice to completely focus on the superficial or the eternal. When we choose to set our affection on things above, we begin to release things from above into this earth. We become a pleasing aroma of heavenly places.

The enemy also understands the law of saturation. If you've been a disciple of Christ for some time now, then the enemy's job is not to tempt you to murder, rob, or even commit adultery. His job is to wear you down over the next decade so that you are not as committed to the things of God as you were before. You are not as vocal about sin as you were before. Or you are not as quick to turn away from inappropriate ads and commercials.

> "...**create** a place where the presence of God is always **welcomed** and **realized**."

Well, what's the remedy to avoiding the enemy's distractions? Saturate in the good stuff! Going without social media for a while—a detox from all of the poisonous atmospheres and information made to wear you down—is a great place to start. Reverse what the devil is doing by saturating in the Word of God, wholesome entertainment, Christian music, etc.

My father in the faith, the late Dr. Carlton Arthurs says 5 essentials make up a true disciple of Christ:

1. The Word
2. Prayer
3. Church
4. Witnessing
5. Giving

Developing an appetite for the 5 essentials helps you become grounded in worship. Although we won't dive into these essentials in this book, we will take the time to show you what can happen as a result of applying these foundations to your everyday life. Before we do that, I want to say that this is not legalism. It is essential. As it says in Matthew 4:4, "...man shall not live by bread alone, but by every word that proceeds out of the mouth of God." In essence, man shall not live by only natural essentials—food, water, shelter, sleep, others, and purpose—but also by spiritual essentials from God.

When you are into the 5 essentials of Christianity, you open yourself up to the Spirit of God coming in and flushing out the toxic life and filling you up with the blessed life. It's in mastering the spiritual fundamentals that we begin developing and strengthening our inner core.

The purpose of saturation in a believer's life is to *create a place where the presence of God is always welcomed and realized.* And when the presence of God is welcomed in your home, it results in peace, protection, and provision.

When talking about creating a place where the presence of God is always welcomed and realized, I have discovered four results:

1. A Change of Atmosphere
2. A Change of Appetite
3. A Change of Altitude
4. A Change of Aroma

A CHANGE OF ATMOSPHERE

The atmosphere changes when we change those things that influence us. Some things are constantly at work in our homes designed to set the general mood. What's the sound in your home? What's coming out of the TV? What's being played on the smart devices? These are the things that are designed to create an atmosphere for good or for evil; for light or darkness; for love or fear.

Entertainment is both a practical and spiritual application but one of utmost importance when creating an atmosphere where God is welcomed. Entertainment is a huge influencer in the average home. The type of music, television, movies, and social media we engage in can and will influence the atmosphere.

Please understand that I am not talking about legalism. Some extremes can be mistaken for the point I'm making—this isn't to say that if you watch sports or check out an occasional decent movie you are evil. What I'm talking about is having things done in moderation while avoiding the appearance of evil (see Romans 12:9).

There are certain movies, TV shows, and music that promote things that God frowns upon. Certain forms of entertainment are designed to dominate the atmosphere, making it an unhealthy place, a place where God is not welcomed. This can be negative information that is piped into our homes that ultimately feeds our spirit-man toxic thoughts which eventually turn into toxic actions that can grieve the Spirit of God.

Put before you the right forms of entertainment, and you'll begin to see the atmosphere become conducive to God's presence (which includes His peace, protection, and provision).

Another key component to experiencing a change of atmosphere is the words that come out of our mouths. We can speak blessings or curses, thanksgiving or complaining, our own opinions, or the Word of God. The choice is up to us as to what type of language we speak in our homes, be it positive or negative.

> "The **choice** is up to us as to what type of **language** we speak in our homes, be it **positive** or **negative**."

Some things need to be cursed in our homes. You have been given authority to control the environment in your home. So, some sights, sounds, and thoughts must be dealt with severely. You must point your finger of authority and say to those ungodly things, "Get out of my house and don't you ever show your ugly face up in here again…in Jesus' name!!" Use your authority. You are seated with Christ in the heavenly realms (see Ephesians 1:19).

Do you have any idols in your home? Is there anything that has been set above the knowledge of God and His things? It has to be pulled down and destroyed so that God's presence is welcomed in your home. Well, you may ask, "What is an idol; what does it look like so that I *can* pull it down?" It can be a tangible object like a car, a house, money, a person, or even a statue made of wood or precious metal. Or it can be an intangible object like a thought, an opinion, a theory, or a way of doing things that is above God's ways of doing things. Whatever the case, God will not share His space with an idol. When God comes, He comes so that peace, prosperity, and protection are exclusively yours and nothing or no one else can take credit for it, only God.

In my home, I have purposed to contend for the presence of God, where He is always welcomed. I want it such that you can come to my home at any time of the day, week, or month, and always sense the presence of God. Does this come by chance? Is it a random act of kindness on God's part, picking our address out of a hat that says we've won the presence lottery? No. This is intentional living. It is contending for the atmosphere. There is a war between me and the culture. The culture is empowered by the god of this world (the devil himself) and his agenda is total domination and ultimately the annihilation of everyone and everything that reminds him of God.

> "**Contend** for the presence of God, where He is **always welcomed**."

The choice is yours as to what you listen to, how you talk, or whether God has been replaced with an idol. Still, if you want the atmosphere to be conducive to the presence of God, then I suggest you simply ask the Lord about it. By His Spirit, He will give you the details of what you should watch, listen to, and engage in within the walls of your home. Isn't this legalism? No, it's intentional living, contending against the culture for the atmosphere in your home, and winning every time! "Behold, I set before you this day a blessing and a curse…" (Deut. 11:26, (KJV).

A CHANGE OF APPETITE

First, I want to establish that appetite is essential to life. My dear friend and pastor, James E. Ward, mentioned that when our appetite for food is waning, it is one of the first signs of something seriously wrong with our bodies. Without a normal appetite for food, we are subject to physical deterioration and ultimately death. Therefore, natural appetite is essential for physical existence and wellness.

Consequently, our spiritual, emotional, and social appetites are like our physical appetites. We need people in our lives who show love and affection as well as facilitate training and affirmation.

Somewhere along life's journey we are introduced to negative appetites that shape new habits and take us to a place where we don't want to go. We find ourselves in need of some major adjustments.

When our appetites change, we no longer have a desire for certain things. Our schedules are impacted by our appetites. Our families are influenced by our appetites. When appetites change, we change spiritually, socially, physiologically, and even financially.

How do you change an appetite? You've heard it said that it takes 21 days to form a habit.

Word of the Lord: God is changing our appetites.
We no longer have a desire for certain things.
Schedules are changing, spiritually we're changing,
socially we're changing, physically we're changing.
You are changing; God is doing a work in you.

There are some things that we want to do for 21 days. Daily confess God's Word. I have to change so I go through 20 minutes of confessions per day. We cannot change by speaking our problems. Therefore, we must say something different than what we see in the natural. The Bible says, "...calling those things that be not as though they are" (Romans 4:17). Form your good habits by speaking the good confessions. Speak over your family, your finances, and your future.

Another way to change your appetite is to "...Abhor what is evil and cling to what is good" (Romans 12:9). When we love what God loves and hate what God hates, we begin to align our appetites with His. One major way of aligning our appetites with God's is by getting into His Word. Read the Bible every day, even if you don't fully understand it. Eventually, you will begin to develop an appetite for more of God's Word.

> "**Consistently** feeding on something over a period of time will eventually become something you **desire** and **enjoy**."

When I try a new vegetable, I have to eat it consistently until I develop a taste for it. This means that over time I will ask for it out of sheer desire. Consistently feeding on something over time will eventually become something you desire and enjoy.

As it is with natural food, so it is with spiritual food. The Word of God, Prayer, Church, Witnessing, and Giving are spiritual things we want to engage in, no matter how foreign it may feel to you at first. It's like those vegetables, over time you will enjoy it.

Motivational speaker and author Terri Savelle Foy says that the goal in developing a habit is making it become a lifestyle. She mentions that the goal of brushing one's teeth isn't to have clean teeth for a while but to make brushing a lifestyle to ensure that you have clean teeth every day for the rest of your life.

Change your appetites to change your habits. Develop good habits to ultimately change your lifestyle.

A CHANGE IN ALTITUDE

As we continue talking about creating a place in which the presence of God is always welcomed and realized, the third result is *A Change of Altitude* and it's extremely important. It can be the determining factor in your moving forward in life or staying still.

Anyone who has been listening to me for the past couple of years has most likely heard me say that I never want to enroll in a school that I cannot graduate from or join an organization that has no plans for promotion for its employees. It's depressing to think about such a scenario. However, that is most people's reality. They are in a cycle of the mundane, a rigorous routine with absolutely no benefits or promises of promotions.

Well, not here and not you! I believe that you are made for promotion; you're wired to graduate from one level to the next.

When you allow the presence of God to change your attitude, you rise above cultural norms. These cultural norms include:

- **Family** – "My dad was an alcoholic, therefore I'm an alcoholic." Or "This is how my family has always done this."
- **Background** – "I grew up in a small town." Or "I grew up on this side of the tracks."
- **Society** – "You know they say he's going to sow his wild oats." Or "You know that's the label they gave me and my generation." Or "This is what I heard on the news…"

Don't get me wrong…the biblical family is God's idea, a faith-centered background is where great foundations can be laid, and a godly family can bring balance and support to a community. But when those things begin to replace God's presence, they become detrimental to us, a subtle snare to the best of us. This includes education, career, boyfriend, girlfriend, new house, new car…all of these are good things in their proper perspective (or altitude). But as soon as we allow them to rise above God, we begin to step into the dimension called idolatry, as I mentioned before. This is simply when we replace God and eternal things with earthly, temporary things. We substitute heavenly things for earthly things. We eat with the chickens when we are made to soar with the eagles!

God is UP! He's in a completely different stratosphere than we are. Colossians 3:2 says, "Set your affection on things above, not on things on the earth." This implies that we have the ability and capacity to focus our attention and our affection on God's things and not let the world's things consume us. We have what it takes to concentrate on God's heart and not the lusts and seductions of this corrupt world system.

Here's more Scripture to illustrate the concept of the believer's potential altitude.

> **For my thoughts are not your thoughts, neither are your ways my ways, saith the Lord. For as the heavens are higher than the earth, so are my ways higher than your ways, and my thoughts than your thoughts (Isaiah 55:8-9, KJV).**

This seems hopeless, unattainable, and impossible to reach. However, God has made a way for us to access His thoughts and His ways. Look at what He says through the apostle Paul:

> **But as it is written: "Eye has not seen, nor ear heard, nor have entered into the heart of man the things which God has prepared for those who love Him." But God has revealed them to us through His Spirit. For the Spirit searches all things, yes, the deep things of God (1 Corinthians 2:10, NKJV).**

We would all be doomed if it weren't for the statement in the middle of this passage, "But God has revealed them to us through His Spirit!" Receiving the Holy Spirit of God is an open invitation to the heart of the Father. This is where secrets are revealed, plans are disclosed, and affirmation is in abundance! We have been given access to God's strategies: His thoughts. We are given access to His character: His ways.

Coming up to this new level in His presence is so worth giving up the temporary pleasures of this world. Moreover, He pulls you up when you simply give Him the attention that He deserves.

A CHANGE OF AROMA

Back in the day, we would take traditional baths (in a tub). My mom would pour the bubble bath liquid into the running water to create the biggest, most dense bubbles ever. This was so much fun for us kids, that we didn't notice, or care, that we were getting clean as long as there were a lot of bubbles and plenty of army action figures.

> "...Whatever you **soak** in, you take on its **aroma**."

Every time we soak in something, we are saturated in it. And whatever we soak in, we take on its aroma. The same is true with the atmosphere you create in your home, dorm room, or space you work in. You are responsible for setting the atmosphere. You get to soak in whatever you choose to soak in, be it wonderfully fragrant or horrifically putrid.

If your goal is to be a sweet-smelling aroma to the Lord and to those who associate with you every day, then wouldn't it be right to soak in something that is pure, holy, righteous, and peaceful? Wouldn't it be the proper investment to listen to music that encourages you? Or, keep company that challenges you to seek the Lord? Or, watch entertainment that promotes holy living? I know I'm starting to meddle, now! But you get my point…soak in good stuff and you'll smell like good stuff!

Your aroma starts in your mind. Whatever you constantly think about, you take on its characteristics. The Scripture that comes to mind is Philippians 4:8. It says,

And now, dear brothers and sisters, one final thing. Fix your thoughts on what is true, and honorable, and right, and pure, and lovely, and admirable. Think about things that are excellent and worthy of praise.

The world is waiting for us to offer a different aroma than what is common to our culture, like hatred, hostility, revenge, entitlement, victimization, greed, and jealousy (to name a few). They are waiting for a soft answer to turn away wrath (Proverbs 15:1). They need exposure to people who turn the other cheek. The world is waiting for real love and not a self-centered imitation.

It behooves us to saturate in the presence of God. Even if you live, work, or play in a hostile environment, you can still bathe in God's presence at the top of the day so that by the time you encounter the first person, you emanate a pleasant aroma that can change their lives. The choice is yours.

PRACTICAL GUIDE

How do I soak in God's presence?

The key here is consistency. And remember, it's not about legalism, but rather developing a trust-relationship with God. Carve out time in your daily routine. If you can't find time, then create time: get up 30 minutes earlier, or use your commute to work. Make an effort and God will meet you halfway.

How do I know when I am giving off a pleasant aroma?

When hostile people begin to respond to you gently, the atmosphere responds to peace and not hostility.

Can I ever arrive at a place where I don't have to do this anymore? No.

Guard your heart above all else, for it determines the course of your life (Proverbs 4:23, NKJV).

4

HEART DIAGNOSIS

There is a place inside each of us that is reserved for all the issues of life. It can hold every major experience, encounter, and chapter of life. It is a secret, secluded place filled with priceless treasures. However, it also remains a very vulnerable place that can only be protected by unseen forces. In the world of the spirit, there must be spiritual guards set in place to protect spiritual assets. Understanding and functioning in these spiritual forces is vitally important to protecting your delicate heart of worship.

Proverbs 4:23 says, "Guard your heart above all else, for it determines the course of your life." In the New Testament, one of our foundational Scriptures puts it like this, "You also be patient. Establish your hearts, for the coming of the Lord is at hand" (James 5:8).

To set up a guard around your heart begins with three things: *Identifying the Treasure, Valuing the Treasure, and Diagnosing the Heart.*

IDENTIFYING THE TREASURE

First, I want to establish that the Keeper of the treasure is Christ in us. He is working through our personalities, our gifts, and our abilities. The indwelling Christ (the Holy Spirit) is our Instructor Who is training and forming our character to properly steward the treasure as well as represent the King and His Kingdom.

The treasure is the light of God's glory in us. It's our ability to be and do good just like Jesus. In 2 Corinthians, the apostle Paul explains this in detail:

> **For it is the God who commanded light to shine out of darkness, who has shone in our hearts to give the light of the knowledge of the glory of God in the face of Jesus Christ (2 Corinthians 4:6).**

We have inside of us the light of God's glory because of Jesus Christ, Who is called the Hope of Glory (see Colossians 1:27). It is important to know that the treasure is sourced out of the glory of God, the place from where all goodness comes. James 1:17 shares, "Every good gift and every perfect gift is from above, and comes down from the Father of lights, with whom is no variableness, neither shadow of turning." Within God's good nature is His propensity to deposit goodness inside of His creation, it's His signature on His masterpiece. Our goodness backs up to His goodness. I like the way the Message Bible translates this passage:

> "...to deposit **goodness** inside of His creation, it's His **signature** on His **masterpiece**."

> **Every desirable and beneficial gift comes out of heaven. The gifts are rivers of light cascading down from the Father of Light. There is nothing deceitful in God, nothing two-faced, nothing fickle. He brought us to life using the true Word, showing us off as the crown of all His creatures (James 1:17, MSG).**

We can rest assured that the Father of Light is the Source of our treasure. He put it there so that we can give Him glory and look like His Son, Jesus.

It's pretty obvious where this treasure is housed: inside of us, our hearts. In 2 Corinthians 4:7 we read, "But we have this treasure in earthen vessels, that the excellence of the power may be of God and not of us."

Some may ask, "Is the heart the blood pump?" or "When you say, 'inside of us', are you talking about next to the lungs or behind the ribcage?" Well, let's look at some more Scripture that speaks to the exact location of the heart and the treasure. Proverbs 20:27 says, "The spirit of man is the candle of the Lord, searching all the inward parts of the belly." So, we see that the heart is not the blood pump we may think of when using this term. The heart simply means CORE. Our bellies house our hearts, and our hearts house the treasure. So, we can safely conclude that everything genuine, authentic, and passionate comes from our core.

> "...Everything **genuine, authentic,** and **passionate** comes from our **core**."

Another Scripture explains the location and motives of the heart-core:

> **A good man out of the good treasure of his heart brings forth good, and an evil man out of the evil treasure of his heart brings forth evil. For out of the abundance of the heart his mouth speaks (Luke 6:45, NKJV).**

VALUING THE TREASURE

To find the true value of a thing, one must invest time into it. While writing this book, I have had to make major decisions as to when to spend time with my family instead of writing. My family is more valuable to me than any literary work I can produce. Ultimately, time well spent is interpreted as high value well placed.

The value of the treasure is determined by both the identification of the treasure and the amount of time invested in the development and care of the treasure. Let's look at what the treasure can manifest as:

> "...**Time** well spent is interpreted as high **value** well placed."

1. Fully developed, world-overcoming faith (1 John 4:4)
2. Supernatural Strength (Philippians 4:13)
3. The Hope of Glory (Colossians 1:27)
4. Integrity of Christ (Galatians 4:19)
5. Desires Fully Met (John 15:4)
6. Guilt-Free Life (Romans 8:1)

The apostle Paul uses an interesting word to describe the treasure in 2 Corinthians 4:7. He writes, "But we have this treasure in earthen vessels, that the excellency of the power may be of God, and not of us." Let's explore this in a different translation:

We now have this light shining in our hearts, but we ourselves are like fragile clay jars containing this great treasure. This makes it clear that our great power is from God, not from ourselves (2 Corinthians 4:7, NLT.)

In this passage, the great treasure is referred to as the great power.

There are 3 dimensions to this power:

- *Power to be witnesses*
- *Power for direction and wisdom*
- *Power to effect change*

Why Hidden Treasure?

No matter how we look at this, the stark reality is that the priceless treasure is hidden in fragile jars of clay. This may seem like a paradox. Or perhaps you may think it's hidden by chance. On the contrary, I believe it is hidden by design.

God displays His genius in putting something of great value into something that appears to be of very little worth for two reasons: First, I truly believe God hides His *best* secrets in the most common, unassuming places just to send the devil on a wild goose chase. The enemy cannot find the next Billy Graham, Mother Teresa, or Nelson Mandela simply because they are hidden, tucked away on some remote island off the coast of Africa, in the dense canopy of trees in the rain forest of South America, or the cornfields of small-town USA. God's massive plan is sometimes packaged in a small, simple parcel (i.e., Moses in a basket, or the Nativity).

> "God's **massive** plan is sometimes packaged in a **small**, **simple** parcel."

Second, I believe the treasure is hidden because it must be protected until the person's character is fully developed to handle the weight of success that the treasure brings. Humble beginnings can keep us humble.

How Does This Apply to Me?

If you are 'hidden'—meaning no one knows your name, or you are not in high demand, or you feel forgotten and invisible—be excited! You are a candidate for God's massive plan. I'm not saying that you will become a superstar worship leader or the next lead pastor of a megachurch. But I *am* saying that in God's eyes, your hidden treasure will be disclosed and celebrated and will ultimately bless many lives in due time.

From hidden to exposed, there's more to this journey than blessing millions with your treasure. "For what shall it profit a man, if he shall gain the whole world, and lose his own soul?" Mark 8:36 says that we don't want to be a public success but a private failure. So, for now, stay hidden as long as it takes so that your godly character and supernatural power are equally balanced and fully developed.

DIAGNOSING THE HEART

Just like we receive a natural diagnosis from the doctor's office, we need a spiritual diagnosis to assess whether our hearts are conditioned to worship God and receive His Word. Here are some steps in performing a self-diagnosis of the heart:

Speaking

> **For whatever is in your heart determines what you say. A good person produces good things from the treasury of a good heart, and an evil person produces evil things from the treasury of an evil heart (Matthew 12:34b-35, NLT.)**

You can locate a person—whether it's their philosophy on life, their political stance, or their religious affiliation—by what comes out of their mouths. I call it 'the talking gauge.' And if you talk to someone long enough—like for instance, over a meal—you might get them to reveal some thoughts from a much deeper place in their heart. However, I've discovered that you can get to the core of a person's beliefs when they are put under an incredible amount of

> "Turning up the **heat** exposes the true motives and **deepest contents** of the heart."

pressure. When the heat is on, the masks come off (no pun intended) and the true heart of a person is exposed. Turning up the heat exposes the true motives and deepest contents of the heart.

Luke 6:45 says, "For out of the abundance of the heart his mouth speaks." When the heart is filled up to a certain level, it will release a lever that triggers the mouth to speak. I am convinced, that we can fill up on enough stuff, whether good or bad, and have it come out of our mouths without any forced effort. It's as simple as breathing. To know what's in your heart, simply check out what's coming out of your mouth.

Believing

Incidentally, 'the talking gauge' also reveals what the individual believes. "For with the heart one believes unto righteousness, and with the mouth confession is made unto salvation" (Romans 10:10). This Scripture gives us the key to where the belief engine is located: "...with the heart one believes..." What we believe is another way to locate the condition of the heart of a person.

Convictions are the collection of beliefs that act as a foundation for which a person stands during intense confrontations or during times of complex decision-making. So, what you believe is what's coming out of your mouth from your heart.

Examining

The Lord is the only one authorized to officially examine the human heart. Consequently, He also gives the most accurate heart diagnosis. Proverbs 21:2 says, "People may be right in their own eyes, but the Lord examines their heart." Another Scripture reveals, "People judge by outward appearance, but the Lord looks at the heart" (1 Samuel 16:7). When being examined, our only obligation is to open up and yield to the Surgeon. We can trust that He knows our hearts. He sees the deepest parts of us and can give us an accurate diagnosis.

Also, we can trust the men and women of God who have been put in our lives to help keep us honest and open. We have a community of people who are in our lives to steer us away from the broad, destructive path, and onto the straight and narrow path that leads to everlasting life (see Matthew 7:13-14).

Prescribing

Our belief systems are birthed out of the heart; it is the place where we trust and obey what we believe. When it's time to speak, we will have overstocked our hearts with what we believe in. This raises the question: How do we overstock our hearts?

Our journey begins with Psalm 45:1. It says, "My heart is overflowing with a good theme; I recite my composition concerning the king; my tongue is the pen of a ready writer." The phrase, "… my tongue is the pen…" shows us how we put the good things in our hearts. Consistently speaking the Word of God writes it on the tablets of the heart. Psalm 119:11 says, "Your word I have hidden in my heart, that I might not sin against You." The word 'hidden' suggests that the Word is pushed deep within our hearts, so deep, that it can't be easily stolen.

The common theme that is understood is that there is *consistently* speaking and thinking on the Word of God that acts as a hammer and chisel against stone. Speaking it over and over forges the deep grooves of text within the surface of our hearts. This is important so that the most dominant script in our hearts is the Word of God, and it cannot be erased.

Take some time to diagnose your heart. Analyze what's coming out of your mouth (especially when under pressure), and take note of what you're believing these days, and whether it lines up with God's Word or not. Being honest with yourself will open you up for God to do a thorough examination. And He will be able to come to accurate conclusions giving way to a proper diagnosis. As a result, you will be on your way to guarding your heart and making worship a lifestyle.

PRACTICAL GUIDE

Setting up a guard around your heart begins with what two things?
1. Identifying the Treasure
2. Valuing the Treasure

We need a self-diagnosis of our hearts. What components do we need to administer a heart diagnosis?
1. Speaking – the language of a person locates what's in their heart
2. Believing
3. Examining
4. Prescribing

THE APPLICATION

5

HEART GUARDS

Guard your heart above all else, for it determines the course of your life (Proverbs 4:23, NLT).

There are so many outside forces warring against our souls, fighting for the first opportunity to demoralize the values that God has meticulously invested in us. The enemy wants to immediately unravel decades of God's perfect tapestry of biblical principles, not to mention desecrate the treasure inside our hearts.

For this reason, we must guard our hearts. We want to keep our hearts tender, pliable, and fully protected in God's hands so that we can worship Him and walk before Him with sincere confidence.

There is an implied question in Proverbs 4:23, "How do I guard my heart?" And how do we guard our hearts when the world around us is in direct opposition to the biblical values we hold dear?

> "Guarding our hearts require **spiritual** substance..."

While studying Proverbs 4:23, I realized there is so much more to the guarding of one's heart than simply avoiding wicked people or hostile situations at all costs. Guarding our hearts requires immaterial substance, spiritual substance. I'll explain…it takes spiritual matter to guard spiritual matter. I can't guard my heart with an ADT security system any more than I can guard against a tornado with a 95mm handgun. More than human willpower, there is a deeper, more effective way to protect our hearts from offense, bitterness, rage, jealousy, envy, strife, and other toxic matters that try to take root in the soil of our hearts.

Listed in the two diagrams below are what I call the Heart Guards. God gave us these irreplaceable weapons in our spiritual arsenal as an answer to the question, "How do I guard my heart?

Additionally, they are not put in order of importance, and this list is not, by far, inexhaustible. They are the Heart Guards I have found to work in my life and am delighted to pass them on to you. They are…

THE HEART GUARDS

THE WORD OF GOD (MEDITATED UPON) – PS. 119:11

TITHE AND OFFERING – MA. 3:10-11; 2 CO. 9:7

FORGIVENESS – MT. 6:14-15; MK. 11:25

PRAISE – PS. 8:2; 113:1-3

THANKSGIVING – PS. 100:4; 141:3

THE WORD OF GOD (SPOKEN) – PS. 45:1; 103:5; PR. 4:20-22

THE BLOOD OF JESUS – HE. 9:14

WISDOM – PR. 4:5-13

THE PEACE OF GOD – PH. 4:7

SERVING OTHERS – GAL. 5:13

FIDELITY – PR. 5:15; 6:26

THE HEART GUARD	GUARDS AGAINST...
The Word of God (Meditated Upon)	ERROR, SIN, and DECEPTION
Tithe and Offering	GREED and POVERTY
Forgiveness	OFFENSE and BITTERNESS
Praise	ACCUSATIONS, CONDEMNATION, and DEPRESSION
Thanksgiving	MURMURING and DELAY
The Word of God (Spoken)	SICKNESS and DISEASE
The Blood of Jesus	DEAD WORKS, DOUBT and UNBELIEF
Wisdom	IGNORANCE and DESTRUCTION
The Peace of God	WORRY, FEAR, and NEGATIVE THINKING
Serving Others	PRIDE, STRIFE, and DESTROYING OTHERS
Fidelity (Holiness)	LUST and CORRUPTION

THE WORD OF GOD (MEDITATED UPON)

We are stabilized when we meditate on the Word of God. Psalm 1:2-3 says, "But his delight is in the law of the Lord, and in His law, he meditates day and night. He shall be like a tree planted by the rivers of water…" Being planted by a river implies stability, fruitfulness, and longevity. The person who has the Word of God as their foundation is set up for success.

A simple definition of meditation is the act of taking what you've learned and thinking about it over and over again so that it becomes a part of your thought processes. It is the process of putting something in the soil of your heart deep enough so that it is never stolen or damaged.

Here's the process of guarding your heart with the Word of God to experience the results that God intends for you to experience:

1. It is the hearing of the preaching of the Word that brings on the appetite to meditate on the Word. (Romans 10:14)
2. Meditating on the Word conditions your spiritual ears for hearing spiritual things. (Romans 10:17b)
3. Hearing the Word of God produces faith. (Romans 10:17a)
4. Faith gives way to obedience. (Hebrews 11)
5. Obeying the Word of God results in seeing what God originally had in mind in that situation or person. It produces stability. (Luke 6:47-49, NLT)

Psalm 119:11 says, "Your word I have hidden in my heart, that I might not sin against You." This is very important in the day in which we live. Hiding the Word of God in our hearts simply means burying it deep within our hearts. The chances of someone (namely the enemy) stealing the Word are very slim.

> "We must **speak** the Word of God in order to **hide** it in our hearts."

When we spend quality time in the Word of God, we are setting up a wall around our hearts to ensure that we are not given to **error or deception.** You may ask, "How do I get the Word of God in my heart?" As I mentioned earlier, Psalm 45:1 says, "My tongue is the pen of a ready writer." The Word of God is put in our hearts through speaking the Word of God from our mouths. Hearing and seeing the Word is not enough. We must speak the Word of God to hide it in our hearts.

Proverbs 3:3b says, "Write them on the tablet of your heart…" When you speak the Word of God, it's like there's a hammer and chisel at work as you speak, carving God's Word with deep grooves. With every syllable, there's another stroke of the chisel chipping away the old negative words, and forging new, life-giving words on the tablet of your heart.

TITHES and OFFERINGS

There's a sobering word in Deuteronomy 8:11-14. It says,

Beware that in your plenty you do not forget the Lord your God and disobey His commands, regulations, and decrees that I am giving you today. For when you have become full and prosperous and have built fine homes to live in, and when your flocks and herds have become very large and your silver and gold have multiplied along with everything else, be careful! Do not become proud at that time and forget the Lord your God, Who rescued you from slavery in the land of Egypt.

Matthew 6:21 says, "For where your treasure is, there your heart will be also." We don't want the treasures of this world to pull our hearts away and consume us with greed and lust for more. Tithes and offerings help regulate the heart. It mainly conditions our hearts to manage wealth. Some people make oaths saying, "When I make more money, then I can afford to pay tithes." The reality is if we can't give what belongs to God, the tithe, while we are bringing in a little money, we will not give it to Him when we are living in abundance. Paying tithes and giving offerings is a way of remembering Who gives us the wealth, the

> "**Tithes** and **offerings**…condition our hearts to manage the wealth."

abundance, the bonuses, the strength to work, etc. (see Deuteronomy 8:18).

This Heart Guard has other benefits as well. We all want our money protected. We long for financial security especially in a time when people are threatened by recessions and economic instability.

I have found that if we pay tithes, a tenth of all of our income, we are placing our money under God's protection. Our money becomes a part of the covenant. But there's more.

Paying tithes and giving offerings can ensure protection around your heart. Again, the Scriptures tell us, "For where your treasure is, there will your heart be also" (Matthew 6:21, KJV). The implication is that if you bring your money under God's protection, your heart is under God's protection. "Protection from what?" you might ask. Your heart is protected from the strong snare of **greed**. This particular temptation is subtle but destructive at its core. The most honest, hard-working people can become selfish, unstable, worldly crooks if their hearts aren't tempered by the safe boundaries of tithes and offerings, giving their finances to Someone greater than themselves. In addition to this, giving offerings is designed to regulate your heart so that you think about others more than you think about yourself.

Giving to people in need keeps you in a position of gratitude. Knowing that what you have is to be distributed to others in need is a gift given to you by your heavenly Father. Giving reminds us that we are nothing more than stewards of God's money.

FORGIVENESS

In the days in which we live, we find it easier to take offense at people and things rather than to forgive. The way someone says something to us, the way the food tastes at the restaurant, and the type of condition the package comes to us in the mail can all contribute to a potential meltdown. Needless to say, there are countless reasons to be offended every day.

We need a heart guard that counters this widespread attack against our heart of worship and peace of mind. It's a matter of sanity and wellness. Where can we find such security to guard our hearts? Matthew 6:14-15 says,

> **And when you pray, make sure you forgive the faults of others so that your Father in heaven will also forgive you. But if you withhold forgiveness from others, your Father withholds forgiveness from you (TPT).**

First, the undertone in this passage is that God gives us the capacity to forgive. He would not tell us to forgive others if He didn't put in us the ability to forgive. This is good news for everyone who calls upon the name of the Lord.

Second, releasing others benefits you more than it does the person you are releasing. You can maintain good health and wellness just by keeping a current log of forgiveness at the top of the day. I'm not a doctor, nor do I claim any medical credentials. But, I do know my own body (as you know yours). And I can tell when I'm holding a grudge how it impacts my physical body. I feel the pressure in my head, the ache in my neck and shoulders, the discomfort in my abdomen. It's all related to not releasing people or scenarios. As soon as I release them, I feel so much better. Likewise, I find that releasing others before they can offend you can reduce stress, lower blood pressure, and help you maintain a healthy attitude throughout your day.

Finally, and most importantly, to forgive is to be forgiven! As we see in Matthew 6:14-15, when we forgive, our heavenly Father will forgive us. God's love is unconditional, but His forgiveness comes with one condition: you must forgive others to receive His forgiveness. It's a sobering yet beautiful exchange.

Forgiveness helps guard your heart against **bitterness and offense**. It is important to guard against bitterness and offense because they can rob you of your health, steal your joy of serving others, and eliminate your opportunities for promotion. So, it's worth it to forgive.

Releasing others of an offense not only releases you into your destiny but keeps your heart tender towards God, empowering you to worship Him freely.

PRAISE

I will bless the Lord at all times; His praise shall continually be in my mouth (Psalm 34:1, KJV).

You have taught children and infants to tell of your strength, silencing your enemies and all who oppose you (Psalm 8:2, NLT).

This part of the security system is very potent. Even through the mouths of children, praise can silence the devil.

Praise guards our hearts against **accusations and condemnation**. The accuser of the brethren has been accusing you both day and night (see Rev. 12:10). All last night he's been coming to the Father saying, "How can you bless this person when they have a wicked past, when they've messed up? How can you use such a person whose life is so corrupt?" Well, when you wake up the next morning and begin your day with praise, you are shutting down all the accusations of the enemy through the night! You are silencing the critical voices in the courtroom of heaven, trumping all those who oppose you and hate you. You say, "Lord, I praise You for Who You are…You are great and greatly to be praised! From the rising of the sun to the going down of the same, the name of the Lord is to be praised! I plead the blood of Jesus in the court of heaven! And I magnify the King of kings and Lord of lords, making Him bigger than my past, my problems, and my enemies!" And you're just getting warmed up!

So, understand that Praise silences the enemy and defuses any trace of accusation and condemnation in your life. Open your mouth and use your Heart Guard of praise to shut down the enemy!

THANKSGIVING

There's so much on this subject in Scripture. I only have room for a few of them. And they are...

- Psalm 26:7 – "…singing a song of thanksgiving and telling of all your wonders."
- Psalm 28:7 – "…I burst out in songs of thanksgiving."
- Psalm 69:30 – "Then I will praise God's name with singing, and I will honor Him with thanksgiving."
- Psalm 95:2 – "Let us come to Him with thanksgiving. Let us sing psalms of praise to Him."
- Psalm 100:4 – "Enter His gates with thanksgiving; go into His courts with praise. Give thanks to Him and praise His name."
- Psalm 107:22 – "Let them offer sacrifices of thanksgiving and sing joyfully about His glorious acts."
- Psalm 116:17 – "I will offer You a sacrifice of thanksgiving and call on the name of the Lord."

We see that thanksgiving is more than just a holiday. It is a lifestyle for the disciple of Christ.

This Heart Guard protects us from **murmuring and delay**. If you want to accelerate some things in your life, then speak the language of the Kingdom of God: Thanksgiving. This language speeds up the manifestations in your life.

Focus on the good that God has done in your life. When we pay close attention to God's goodness and keep a grateful attitude,

> "A **byproduct** of thanksgiving is it makes you **attractive**!"

we become a homing device for more goodness. A byproduct of thanksgiving is it makes you attractive!

No more complaining. As Kent Henry, a pioneering worship leader of the '80s and '90s, says, "Replace the spirit of complaining with the spirit of thanksgiving." We need this Heart Guard so that we can accelerate the promises of God in our lives, and guard against murmuring and delay.

THE WORD OF GOD (SPOKEN)

Our lives are flooded with words. From social media, news media, coworkers, family members, and friends, we are inundated with everyone's opinion of how things should be. Everyone is a professional critic, now. They know what a family is supposed to be like; a marriage, raising children, what's right and wrong, what you should and should not believe. Society at large no longer honors the privacy of one's values, experiences, and successful results.

We live in a world that feels life can be lived without any divine assistance and no supernatural intervention. We have been conditioned to live our lives without God and His Word.

Well, I refuse to leave my life up to chance. Neither do I want a godless society dictating to me how things should be: my marriage, my family, the raising of my children, my home, my values, etc.

Societies change. People change. Opinions change with the latest thought patterns and ideologies. I often say that society is fickle: in the '70s smoking was socially acceptable (even on airplanes), while homosexuality was taboo. Now, smoking is banned in all public buildings and all commercial flights, and homosexuality is not only accepted, it's celebrated in the public squares!

So, excuse me if I don't build my life on something that will change in the next 10 years, leaving my family confused. Rather, I want to build my life on something that will never pass away. I want to decree a thing and see the results in my own family (see Job 22).

The Bible says that we are kings and priests unto our God (Revelation 1:6; 5:10). As a king, I can decree out of my mouth the results I want in my life. I choose to speak the Word of God.

Speaking the Word of God guards our hearts against **sickness and disease** and any other evil that tries to come against us. Once we speak the Word of God, it doesn't mean that all evil goes away and never returns. However, it sets up a wall around our hearts against negative thoughts and words, keeping them from setting up permanent residency there. As the saying goes, "Birds will fly over your head, but you can stop them from making a nest in your hair."

> "I want to **build** my life on something that will never pass away."

Ultimately, we shape our world through our words. You have the power and the authority to speak over your world. And the best way to do that is by getting by yourself, in your prayer time, and begin speaking what you desire based upon the Word of God. You can speak over your children, your loved ones, your career, your future, etc. We don't want to say what we currently see with our natural eyes. We want to speak the Word of God, something that will never pass away. Or like I always say, "The Word of God has no shelf life. It's eternal."

By speaking the Word of God, you are saying what God says. You are decreeing what God has already decreed from heaven. No sickness, disease, poverty, or sin can penetrate the heavy-duty Heart Guard of the Word of God Spoken.

THE BLOOD OF JESUS

Hebrews 9:13-14 says, "Under the old system, the blood of goats and bulls and the ashes of a heifer could cleanse people's bodies from ceremonial impurity. Just think how much more the blood of Christ will purify our consciences from sinful deeds so that we can worship the living God." Our consciences need cleansing from the stain of sinful thoughts and patterns of this world "so that we can worship the living God."

In Romans 12:2 we see that there are behaviors and customs of this world that we should not copy. When we have lived a life with worldly behaviors and customs long enough, we are blemished and marked by them, making us slaves to them.

> "The precious Blood of Jesus (gives) us the **audacity** to stand before God and act as if we've never sinned."

In biblical times (particularly the Old Testament), the custom of turning a man into a slave for life required hammering an awl into the ear of the slave by the master. The slave chose to remain a servant to his master permanently.

As the Scriptures say, "Behold, I was brought forth in iniquity, and in sin my mother conceived me." Sin is a hard taskmaster, driving people into intense slavery with no hopes of ever being set free. However...

There is a power that is more potent than the grip of sin, a force more intense than the mark of iniquity in our hearts. The BLOOD of Christ is the most incredible solution that rids us of the stain of sin and its grip on our lives. It is the precious Blood of Jesus that washes us clean, giving us the audacity to stand before God and act as if we've never sinned.

The Blood of Jesus guards our hearts against **dead works, doubt, and unbelief.** James 2:20 says that "faith without works is dead." If we are producing dead works, our faith isn't working. In essence, we are operating in doubt and unbelief when all we see are dead works. It is the Blood that gives us a clean slate, pressing the reset button of the heart.

> What can wash away my sin?
> Nothing but the blood of Jesus.
> What can make me whole again?
> Nothing but the blood of Jesus.
> Oh, precious is the flow
> That makes me white as snow
> No other fount I know
> Nothing but the blood of Jesus.

This great hymn of the faith is true. The Blood of Jesus has the power to wash clean and make whole. The process of cleansing one's conscience is understood to include the scrubbing away of past thought patterns and habits that result in negative behaviors. However, it's not just a cleaning service. It's a repair shop. The Blood takes care of it all. It prepares the conscience for a fresh start. The restoration of the soul is underway when the Blood has been applied to the conscience. It has the power to save, heal, deliver, restore, and give you access to God's presence and all of God's promises. Hebrews 10:19 says, "And so, dear brothers and sisters, we can boldly enter heaven's Most Holy Place because of the blood of Jesus." The phrase "Most Holy Place" is the place of worship, it is where you meet with God. This is made possible only by the precious blood of Jesus!

WISDOM

When talking about guarding our hearts, we know that there's an enemy that is set on keeping us in ignorance of the Word of God. The enemy's goal is to make the things of God of very little value, or of no value at all.

Scripture tells us the fear of the Lord is the beginning of wisdom (Psalm 111:10). To fear the Lord is to place the highest value upon Him and His things. A reverential fear of God simply means that we are in awe of Him.

Wisdom is not the same as knowledge or understanding. You can have a person filled with knowledge but lacking in wisdom. Just like you can have someone filled with understanding but never act on that understanding. My pastor, James E. Ward, says that we can love God with all our hearts and still live a dysfunctional life. We need the wisdom of God to be successful in life.

The benefits of applied wisdom far outweigh the value of gold and silver. Proverbs 8:6 says, "The meaning of my words will release within you revelation for you to reign in life." Everyone wants to reign in life. But wisdom is how to begin the journey to reigning.

A good biblical way of defining wisdom is the God-given ability to judge between what's right and wrong; acknowledging that it was the Creator who empowers us to apply knowledge and understanding to everyday life.

Understanding and applying what we know (particularly from God's Word) is keeping us on the path of wisdom. Proverbs is packed with wisdom concepts. In Proverbs 4:6 it says, "Don't turn your back on wisdom, for she will protect you. Love her, and she will guard you." What does wisdom protect and guard you from? It protects your heart from **ignorance and destruction**.

In The Passion Translation, Proverbs 8:13 says, "Wisdom pours into you when you begin to hate every form of evil in your life, for that's what worship and fearing God is all about." If we want to have an influx of wisdom without measure, it all begins with us hating every form of evil in our lives. There is a balancing act for the believer: "Hate evil and love what is good" (Amos 5:15, NLT). Another Scripture says, "Let love be without hypocrisy. Abhor what is evil. Cling to what is good" (Romans 12:9, NKJV).

It's time to embrace wisdom. Let us keep it close to our hearts so that we remain protected from anything that can keep us in ignorance or ultimately destroy us.

THE PEACE OF GOD

Philippians 4:7 says, "Then you will experience God's peace, which exceeds anything we can understand. His peace will guard your hearts and minds as you live in Christ Jesus." It doesn't get any clearer than that! God's peace is available to anyone who needs it. However, we must explore how this is made possible.

As we look at the verses before verse 7, we discover the 'how' behind the peace of God. Verse 6 reads, "Don't worry about anything; instead, pray about everything. Tell God what you need, and thank him for all he has done." This also is very clear. We will experience God's peace as we follow these simple instructions:

1. **Don't worry** about anything – choose to trust in God, making Him bigger than your problems
2. **Pray** about everything – come to God with your challenges, struggles, and trials, making Him the Lord of your life
3. **Tell God** what you need – ask Him for the answer to your problems, making Him the source of your every need
4. **Thank Him** for all He has done – keep things in proper perspective; from the simple to the complex, He is always good; making thanksgiving a lifestyle

The peace of God is so potent that it not only guards our hearts but also guards our minds as we stay hidden in Christ Jesus. What's so important about this double duty? The heart is the final chamber of our responses to life's issues. The mind, however, is the second chamber of our existence. Well, you may ask, "What's the first chamber?" The eyes, the ears, and the mouth are where everything is introduced. What you see, what you hear, and what you say out of your mouth determine what enters the second chamber, the mind.

People find it difficult to filter the flood of information coming in at such a rapid pace every day, all day. It's no wonder many are suffering from anxiety, mental illness, stress, depression, and much more. There is a breakdown in the filtering system of peace. We can't keep from seeing, hearing, and speaking. Neither should we pluck out our eyes, muffle our ears, and go on vocal rest forever! No. God has made a way for us to experience peace in our minds as well as our hearts.

Remember this is **God's peace** at work inside of us 24/7. His peace is a filter and a guard. It works overtime to ensure that we never experience a meltdown or a blowup!

What does His peace guard your heart against? It guards your heart against **worry, fear, and negative thinking**. These are heavy-hitting attacks against our fragile hearts. So, our means of defense have to be of greater strength. Peace is a powerful force that God has given us as we keep our trust in Him. Isaiah 26:3 says, "You will keep in perfect peace all who trust in you, all whose thoughts are fixed on you!" Perfect peace comes with perfect trust.

SERVING OTHERS

For you have been called to live in freedom, my brothers and sisters. But don't use your freedom to satisfy your sinful nature. Instead, use your freedom to serve one another in love.

Galatians 5:13 paints a clear picture of the purpose of our freedom in Christ. True freedom is for the sole purpose of serving each other in the spirit of love. Serving others helps keep us in the mindset of "it's not always about me."

Sometimes to find out what something *is* we must begin with what it *is not*. Service to others doesn't mean our focus is on their response to our service. The ones we serve aren't our primary focus. True service to others should be centered on Christ. Regarding how we should serve, the apostle Paul in Ephesians 6:7 says, "Work with enthusiasm, as though you were working for the Lord rather than for people." To work for people involves toil, obligation, stress, and worry. To work for God involves trust, peace, and rest.

The best service is when someone serves God through serving others. When the focus is on pleasing God while serving others, no one can discourage, distract, derail, or divide your loyalty. If pleasing God is the aim, then you can't fail.

Serving others guards our hearts against **pride, strife, and destroying others.**

FIDELITY

You might ask the question, "What does this have to do with guarding my heart?" Well, the subject of fidelity is the litmus test of the health of a marriage. To better understand why this is so important regarding the heart, let's look at what Jesus says in Matthew 5:28.

> **But I say, anyone who even looks at a woman with lust has already committed adultery with her in his heart.**

The success or failure of a marriage begins in the privacy of one's heart. In essence, Jesus says the act of adultery begins with looking upon a woman with lust by allowing the thoughts of undressing her or seeing yourself sleeping with her to run loose in your mind. Once you let these thoughts go without restraint, you are committing the sin of adultery before the physical act of committing adultery. No mature consenting adult can honestly say, "I stumbled onto this act of sexual sin." The act of adultery began in the mind.

It takes the conditioning of the mind to reject the lustful thoughts and images that can give way to acting out what has been meditated upon. As the saying goes, "You are what you eat." Well, I say, "You are what you consistently think about!" Proverbs 23:7 says, "As he thinks in his heart, so is he." Your most dominant thought can potentially become a stronghold that leads you down a path of destruction of your marriage, your family, and your lifestyle of worshiping God.

Fidelity begins with the resolve that I will not let my eyes wander. I will "[cast] down imagination and every high thing that exalts itself against the knowledge of God, and [I] bring into captivity every thought to the obedience of Christ" (2 Corinthians 10:5).

A mindset of fidelity guards our hearts against **lust and corruption**. But there's more to casting down thoughts. There is a physical connection to the spiritual realities.

AND ANOTHER THING...

We must understand that there is more to worship than the unseen things like the heart, the spirit man, or the inner man. There is another element called holiness. Holiness is being set apart for God's use. But what does it mean to be holy in the day in which we live? What does holiness look like every day?

We each have a physical body, the place where the five senses are contained. When it comes to true worship, we want to not only focus on the heart. We should also consider the body. When you come before the Lord in worship, you are bringing your whole being, including your body. It says in Psalm 15:1, "Who may worship in your sanctuary, Lord? Who may enter Your presence on Your holy hill?" And again, in Psalm 24:3, "Who may climb the mountain of the Lord? Who may stand in his holy place?"

It sums it all up in chapter 15 verse 2 and chapter 24 and verse 4. It says,

Those who lead blameless lives and do what is right...

Only those whose hands and hearts are pure...

Living holy backs up to living a blameless life, living a life that is pleasing to the Lord. The bad news is that you can't do this. The good news, however, is that with God's help, you can live a blameless life. "How?" you may ask. Let's go back to the Word of God.

Romans 12:1 says, "...I plead with you to give your bodies to God because of all he has done for you. Let them be a living sacrifice—the kind he will find acceptable. This is truly the way to worship him." Worshipping the Lord in His sanctuary is more than dressing up on a Sunday morning, singing nice songs, and impressing people with a polished worship set and skillful talent. Worship becomes who you are physically as well as spiritually. Let's explore this further.

When we present our bodies to God as a living sacrifice, we begin the process of being kept blameless. In essence, your body is the seed, and your harvest is you being kept blameless. This is found in 1 Thessalonians 5:23. It says,

Now may the God of peace make you holy in every way and may your whole spirit and soul and body be kept blameless until our Lord Jesus Christ comes again.

This Scripture suggests that God can make you holy. He can set you apart in every way. And when God makes you holy, you are holy; there's no discussion and no debate.

We can count on this process because it backs up to a promise. Verse 24 says, "God will make this happen, for he who calls you is faithful." You sow the seed, your body, and He helps you to live a blameless life. So, living a blameless life backs up to living a surrendered life, giving God your physical body. Today, offer God your hands, your feet, your mouth, your eyes.

In 1 Corinthians 6:19-20, we see some interesting thoughts regarding our bodies as an offering to the Lord.

Don't you realize that your body is the temple of the Holy Spirit, who lives in you and was given to you by God? You do not belong to yourself, [20] for God bought you with a high price. So you must honor God with your body.

Therefore, worship is...
- An Aroma vs. an act
- A Sacrifice vs. a skill set
- A Lifestyle vs. a livelihood

AN AROMA VS. AN ACT

First, our focus isn't on presenting our bodies as much as it is on the One we're presenting it to and the aroma it produces. It is the aroma of our lives that rises to God. It's more than what comes from our mouths. It's all about what emanates from our lives of gratitude.

I am a worship leader and I believe in singing praises to God and expressing my love to Him from the stage. But that's not worship. Worship is what I did Monday through Saturday. Worship is being honest with my kids and telling them when I miss it. Worship to God is how I treat my colleagues on my job. Worship is how I treat my wife behind closed doors. The stage is not worship. It is simply the overflow of a life lived before God. Am I perfect? No. But I surrender this body to God. So, your life is worship to God, an aroma that comes up to Him.

A SACRIFICE VS. A SKILL SET

We are bringing our bodies to God as a living sacrifice. Are we perfect? No. Do we have flaws? Yes. Yet, the sacrifice that God wants is our bodies. The same body that we used for sin, we now offer it to God as a living sacrifice.

Many of us (meaning musicians, singers, etc.) have mastered our musicianship. And there is a place for skill as it relates to playing and singing to the Lord. He deserves our best so, we hone our skills and maintain the quality of our craft. This is very appropriate as Scripture says, "Sing a new song of praise to him; play skillfully on the harp, and sing with joy" (Psalm 33:3). However, the skill set for God should never replace the sacrifice to God. In other words, we want to keep the top priority at the top: offering our lives to God and then our skill sets.

> "...the **skill set** for God should never replace the **sacrifice** to God."

A LIFESTYLE VS. A LIVELIHOOD

Worship is what we offer to God 24/7. As a musician or worship leader, it was never about the money. Before I was hired to lead worship, for years I played and sang at my dad's church for free. I didn't get hired until after I trained under Tim and Monica Amstutz, Music Ministries Directors at Oral Roberts University. It was during this time that I received the information and revelation on the balance between living a lifestyle of worship versus having a job in a church (or university). The line can be very thin, especially in our current era.

The church has made the mistake of creating a culture of hirelings and not a culture of making disciples of Christ among its musicians. The skill set took priority over sonship. We were saying to the musician, "You play for us, we pay you, and no one watches for your soul." Sadly, the church musician has become a vagabond, a wanderer without direction, protection, and accountability. Their lives are no different than that of a secular musician, who makes his livelihood in erotic nightclubs, hostile bars, and worldly concerts. Their lives are a wreck while they play for the church. They sit in the house of God while their houses are in shambles. They minister to the Bride of Christ while their marriages are on the rocks!

I want to pass on to you what's been given to me: this doesn't have to be the case. You can be a follower of Christ who happens to be an amazing musician. You can be a disciple of Christ who happens to sing skillfully.

The Lord loves us so much that He not only wants us to have life but to have it "…in abundance (to the full, till it overflows)" (John 10:10b, AMPC). Not only will our lives naturally benefit from the church, but our lives can also spiritually benefit from the church. Our lifestyles can flourish while we work for the church.

PRACTICAL GUIDE

Guarding our hearts requires spiritual substance. The Heart Guards are the security system of the inner man. They are:

1. The Word of God (Meditated Upon)
2. Tithe and Offering
3. Forgiveness
4. Praise
5. Thanksgiving
6. The Word of God (Spoken)
7. The Blood of Jesus
8. Wisdom
9. The Peace of God
10. Serving Others
11. Fidelity

6

PERSONAL PRAYER ALTAR

God is a generational God. He wants us to pass on to the next generation the proper way to worship Him, to offer Him the sacrifice of praise from a life committed to Him.

Psalm 145: "One generation shall praise Thy works to another, and shall declare Thy mighty acts." It's up to us to have a personal intimate relationship with Jesus. And then we pass it on to our children. We testify to the next generation of what the Lord has done in our lives. That's our responsibility.

> "…your house is a **house of prayer** for all nations."

Isaiah 56:7 says, "I will bring them to my holy mountain, Jerusalem. And I will fill them with joy in my house of prayer. I will accept their burnt offerings and sacrifices because my temple will be called a house of prayer for all nations." This is where you live; your house is a house of prayer for all nations. It's more than just bricks and mortar; or where you sleep, eat, and watch TV. Your house is a miniature church. When someone comes into your house they should sense the peace and presence of God. They don't want to leave your home because of the presence of God. Your house is the hallowed ground because of Who lives inside of you.

Your house is a portal from earth to heaven; a place where angels ascend and descend. There's Kingdom business that happens in your house. If you haven't figured it out by now, your house is more than just a house!

To expose the next generation to the presence of God, we cannot leave it up to the local church, Christian TV programming, or even to chance. Here are some practical ways to expose our children to the presence of God:

1. Establish a Prayer Altar in Our Homes
2. Lead by Example (my feet are the first to hit the floor)
3. The Offering (how to bring an offering to the Lord)

THE PERSONAL PRAYER ALTAR

Disclaimer:

This is NOT legalism. It's a spiritual essential. It is sourced out of a love relationship with God. We can't wait to spend time in His presence. Another word we can use to describe our time with God is 'delight.' And if you don't have it, ask for it. The Holy Spirit says through the apostle Paul in Philippians 2:13,
"God is working in you, giving you the desire and the power to do what pleases Him." Just ask Him.

Priorities: Set a specific place and time where you are going to spend time with God, seek Him, and draw His presence into your home.

Components of the Prayer Altar:

1. The Word of God (giving it first place and final authority in our lives)
2. Praise and Worship (a place where you magnify the Lord and hallow His name audibly) (a lot of voices that are decreeing while we are sleeping)

3. Repentance (this is when we repent for every negative word, action, motive, and thought)
4. Intercession and Confession

THE WORD OF GOD

There must be a time for reading the Word at the altar so that your soul can be saturated in the wisdom, truth, and counsel of God (*Prayer Altars*, by John Mulinde and Mark Daniel; World Trumpet Mission Publishing, 2013).

We need large portions of the Word being poured into us because of the large portion of negative information that's coming to us. We get it from all sides. People are very vocal about what they are against, giving their opinions and interpretations of how they feel things should be. They are pointing out the failures and flaws of everyone and everyone else has become a professional critic.

We need the Word of God to come into our hearts and flush out all the negative stuff. The Word of God is like water to wash us clean. It washes us of the filth of the world. It washes us of the filthy atmospheres. Have you ever been in a nasty atmosphere? Well, the Word has a way of washing over your soul and cleansing you of the negative atmospheres. My pastor, Pastor James Ward, Jr., says, "The Word of God convicts us as we leave the house, and cleanses us when we return."

> "Before anyone else can speak over my family, I speak over my family the **Word of God**."

As the apostle Paul addresses the behavior of the Christian household in Ephesians, he uses the analogy of water when he explains the roles of the husband and how he should relate to his wife. He writes, "Husbands, love your wives, even as Christ also loved the church and gave Himself for it; that He might sanctify and cleanse it with the washing of water by the Word."

Heads of households are given their biblical right and authority to cleanse their families of the filth of this world. Before anyone else can speak over my family, I speak over my family the Word of the Lord.

As we speak the Word of God, we simultaneously cancel the negative words spoken over us. In the prayer altar, we are allowed to make deposits into our souls during peacetime. And when the battle begins, we have the right word at the right time.

PRAISE and WORSHIP

We draw our focus and attention to the Lord, then continue in an attitude of worship and praise. We do this until we eliminate whatever is trying to steal our focus and keep our hearts from becoming fixed on Christ.

The enemy's job is to steal, kill, and destroy (John 10:10). He tries to steal your focus, kill your passion, and destroy your devotion to the Lord. He comes through a text or a phone call, it can be anything. With technology, we constantly have things popping up on our devices (one major reason I have resorted to the conventional Bible when I do a personal Bible study).

We are drawing the presence of God through Praise and Worship. It helps us keep our focus during our prayer altar. I have found that through hallowing the name of the Lord, we draw the presence of God into our homes. This is the time we bring our best to the Lord. It's called the sacrifice of praise.

REPENTANCE

Contrary to popular belief, repentance isn't a negative spiritual discipline. It is designed to help us draw closer to God and move away from self-destruction. We bear our souls to the Lord and repent for every negative word, action, motive, and thought. And after we have repented, let's not forget a very important part that many Christians forget: receive your forgiveness by faith. We don't want to stay and wallow in repentance. This can lead to depression, oppression, and 'woe is me' syndrome. If left unchecked, repentance can cause our weaknesses to become the focus and not His strength. Rather, we keep the proper perspective by saying, "Lord, I know I'm a hot mess, I know I'm not worthy, I know I don't measure up. But God, I receive Your forgiveness by faith. I know that You've forgiven me. You blotted out my transgressions, and all You told me to do is confess my sins and You are faithful and just to forgive me of my sins and to cleanse me from all unrighteousness. So, God, I receive my forgiveness" (Psalm 51:1; 1 John 1:9).

We are also able to forgive others. We can release others just like we've been forgiven. And this is the part of repentance that can be challenging because it's easier to hold a grudge than it is to release someone. It's unnatural to release people because of our fallen world. Especially in our culture, it's easy to unfriend someone who has done or spoken something against you. But in the personal prayer altar, you want to release people because you have been released. The only leverage with which we have to forgive others is our having been forgiven! Your heart is now conditioned for worship. You are ready for the next level.

INTERCESSION

It's always appropriate to pray for ourselves. However, we want to use this time to intercede for others, to hold God's hand while we hold someone else's hand in need.

I have come to enjoy this part of the prayer altar. I get to bring others into this space simply by praying for them and calling their names before God. As I mentioned before, we are holding their hands as we hold God's hand. These are people who may not know how to pray for themselves. They may not know how to call upon the name of the Lord. But what we do is stand in the gap for them. I'm bearing their burden right now (Galatians 6:2).

God will ignite a flame in us that moves us from local needs to global needs. You will find this to be true as you engage in prayer for others. It will progress from "me and mine" to neighborhoods, cities, regions, and nations. You may be reading this book and sense God tugging at your heart because of a specific grace and calling on your life for intercession. There's a burning in your soul to pray for others who cannot pray for themselves. Let me say God is elevating you to the next level of intercession. You will begin to see faces, regions, and cities. Individual people will come to your mind during your prayer time. Some you will know and some you may not know. But you can rest assured that it's time to pray for this individual. That's the reason they keep coming to your mind; you see their face every time you pray. They don't have the sense to do it right now, but you're going to cry out to God on their behalf.

CONFESSIONS (Job 22:25-28)

It is important to say what we want. We shape our world through our words. You have the power and the authority to speak over your world. So, the best way to do that is behind the scenes, in your prayer time.

You can speak over your spouse, your children, your home, and your destiny. You're not saying what you see with your natural eyes. Rather, you are saying what God says about it. We are decreeing the Word of the Lord.

I have confessions for my wife, my children, my extended family, our health, our prosperity, etc. I refuse to leave my future up to chance (to someone else's opinion as to what my family and future should look like).

We are given the authority to speak into our children's lives. This is the type of person they are going to marry, this is how they are going to behave, these are the grades they are going to receive, and these are the friends they are going to attract. Nothing is left to chance. Everything is intentional. It's already spoken into the atmosphere.

Private confessions bring public breakthroughs.

PRACTICAL GUIDE

What are the ways we can expose our children to the presence of God?

- Establish a Prayer Altar in Our Homes
- Lead by Example (my feet are the first to hit the floor)
- The Offering (how to bring an offering to the Lord)

What are the components of the Prayer Altar?

- The Word of God
- Praise and Worship
- Repentance
- Intercession and Confession

7

PUT YOUR HEART INTO IT

Worship is bringing God an offering (see Genesis 22:5). There are different types of offerings we bring to the Lord: offerings of money, time, worship, etc. But there is only *one way* to bring an offering to the Lord: bring your best! Bring Him your best and you'll bring it in faith and confidence.

What does it mean to give God your best? There are a few thoughts I want to share with you to help you condition your heart to give God your best. They are:

1. The Right Attitude
2. The Right Motive
3. The Right Ingredients
4. The Right Results

THE RIGHT ATTITUDE

Who wants to have a party thrown for them, only to have everyone show up out of duty or obligation? Psalm 100:2 says, "Serve the Lord with gladness…" This depicts the condition of the heart. The Lord desires that whatever we do for Him, we do it with enthusiasm.

Another Scripture says, "…serve the Lord your God with joy and gladness of heart, for the abundance of everything…" (Deuteronomy 28:47, NKJV). Now, if we keep this Scripture in its proper context, it's in regards to the curse that results when not serving the Lord with joy and gladness. However, we are not like that. You are reading this book because you are one of those who have decided to serve the Lord with enthusiasm! God wants gladness of heart when we come to Him.

At a five-star restaurant, you expect a certain level of service. You are paying for the tremendous attention to detail, an experience that results in you saying to yourself, "I am one valued customer." Even at a greasy-spoon diner, at the very least, you expect service with a smile. So, how much more for the King of kings? He deserves the right attitude every time.

> "Bring (God) your best and you'll bring it in **faith** and **confidence**."

Psalm 4:5 says, "Offer sacrifices in the right spirit, and trust the Lord." I found a secret in knowing how to offer sacrifices in the right spirit…it's in reversing this Scripture to say, "When you trust the Lord, you can offer sacrifices in the right spirit." Trusting in Him can guarantee the right motives for your offering (more on this in a moment).

When it comes to monetary gifts, we no longer have to throw our offerings in the bucket, bidding them farewell. No, we get to come rejoicing in the fact that God has given us gainful employment, strength to work, and the abundance of all things! One familiar Scripture that comes to mind is 2 Corinthians 9:7, "…for God loves a cheerful giver." Here it is again, God desiring that we come to Him with the right attitude. We aren't glad because someone told us to be glad. Gladness is a byproduct of our gratitude for all He has done for us. We want to come to God with joy and gladness of heart because He has simply been so good to us!

Ultimately, we are invited to God's party. The least we can do is show up with a smile (both on our faces and in our hearts). But let's go beyond that. Let's show up with our best. Our attitudes will eventually impact our hearts, which should result in generous gifts, quality devotion, and affectionate worship.

THE RIGHT MOTIVE

When looking at the heart behind the offering, we must explore the very first offering recorded in Scripture: the offerings of Cain and Abel. In Genesis 4:1-10, we see that the two sons of Adam offer the Lord an offering. The implication here is that Adam has instructed his sons in the components of a proper sacrifice to the Lord. He educated them in God's desires for an appropriate offering: our best.

The story of Cain and Abel is not based on the offering (although it has a lot to do with it). Neither is it centered on occupations like sheep herding or agriculture. Rather, it speaks of the obedience of one son and the disobedience of the other son.

Abel purposes in his heart to obey his father by giving God the best of his flock; a gift fit for a king. This offering comes from a tender heart of relationship, fellowship, and obedience.

However, Cain disregards his father's instructions and gives from the last of his harvest. He keeps the best for himself and gives the Lord something unfit to eat, much less for a king. His offering comes from a hardened heart of duty, obligation, and ultimately, disobedience.

God accepts worship from a heart that gives Him the best. However, the engine behind our best offerings should come from a trust relationship built upon the foundation of love and obedience to God's instructions. A perfect example of this is found in the entire chapter of Psalm 119. Nearly every verse, all 176 of them, speaks of love for God's Word. David not only likes God's Word; he loves and delights in God's Word.

Gratitude drives us to give our best every time. We move from the obligation zone into the delightful zone when we are motivated by a grateful heart. Ultimately, if it's not done from a grateful heart, keep your offering and your service to the Lord. It is better to *not* do something when your heart isn't in it than to do something half-heartedly. God loves a cheerful giver. He is looking for people who serve when motivated by love for the Recipient of the gift.

Love for God, I'm talking true gratitude, is our motive for giving our best to God. Genuine love drives out fear. The Scriptures say, "There is no fear in love, but perfect love casts out fear..." (1 John 4:18). When you get rid of fear, you get rid of insecurities, competition, comparisons, pride, and covetousness. It's time to let God's love motivate us to give our best!

> "It is better to **NOT** do something when your heart isn't in it, than to do something **half-heartedly.**"

We can safely conclude that love and obedience are the motivating factors to giving our best to the Lord. Isaiah 1:19 says, "If you are willing and obedient, you shall eat the good of the land." Another Scripture ties it all together. Look at what Jesus says in John 15:10.

> **When you obey my commandments, you remain in my love, just as I obey my Father's commandments and remain in his love.**

THE RIGHT INGREDIENTS

Have you ever baked something only to find out that you missed one key ingredient? Well, it doesn't take long to find out what's missing, especially if you've baked this food several times before. Through the years I have learned that offering God our best requires some basic ingredients. Let's begin with the core ingredients that make up an offering:

- What's in your hand – Gifts | Talents | Life's Work
- Humility – Broken | Stripped of Self
- Honoring – Total Focus on the Recipient of the Gift

What's in your hand: Giving our best back up to the stuff you currently have in your hands. Moses had a staff. Elijah used the bottle of oil. Jesus used the six large clay pots of water to perform His first miracle recorded in Scripture. The ingredients used for giving your best are now within your reach. You don't have to look far to find the right tools. God has placed a lot inside of you to get the job done. Second Corinthians 4:7 says, "But we have this treasure in earthen vessels, that the excellency of the power may be of God, and not of us."

Humility (James 4:10): You do not consider yourself when giving your best. You are stripped of self-importance, self-seeking, self-reliance, and self-righteousness. You don't consider the amount it will cost you because you have resolved that He is worth it. You can say, "Take away my title, take all my trophies, and you can have the kingdom I've built. Just don't take the Source of my life and joy and peace! Just give me Jesus."

Honoring (Proverbs 3:9): The Recipient of the offering is your primary focus. You feel that the One on whom you lavish your gift is deserving of your best. The payoff for giving honor is that you become a vessel of honor or an honorable person (the law of reciprocity).

Three other components make up the offering (or sacrifice). Let's look at Genesis 22:5-7. In it, we see the other elements that make an offering of worship to the Lord:

- The Wood – Your Body (Romans 12:1)
- The Fire – The Holy Spirit | Conviction | The Voice
- The Lamb – The Will | The Surrendered Life

THE RIGHT RESULTS

What can we expect out of a life that is giving God their best every time? I believe that you can expect the following:

- Consistency
- Faithfulness
- Confidence
- Celebration of Others
- Sincerity
- Thankfulness

Giving your best results in Consistency: We purpose in our hearts to give 100 percent every time. Whether we're on a stage or in a living room, we give 100 percent every time we open our mouths and come into the presence of God. Purpose in your heart to give your best, whether there are 25 people in the audience or 25,000 people in the stadium!

Giving your best results in Faithfulness: We keep showing up, ready to serve at any time. Consequently, our punctuality reflects the value we place on the One we serve. The audience of ONE is the Lord Himself. Colossians 3:23 says, "And whatever you do, do it heartily, as to the Lord, and not unto men."

Giving your best results in Confidence: We dare to come before the King with boldness and without reservations because we know we have given our absolute best.

Giving your best results in the Celebration of Others: We have no comparisons or competitions. There's no such thing as coveting each other's gifts in an atmosphere where everyone is celebrated. Giving God your best helps you stay in your lane, there's a sense of personal fulfillment so that you can focus on others.

Giving your best results in Sincerity: We dig deep to draw from a genuine place; no more masks (John 4:23-24). We know that it doesn't come from a superficial place. If you're reading this book, you are most likely done with surface worship. We want to experience worship from a deeper place, a place where we can be real with God and He can reveal more of Himself to us. During peacetime, we must make up our minds to give God our best during the heat of the battle. It's only then that we can draw from a genuine place when everything around us is telling us to remain on the surface.

Giving your best results in Thankfulness (Psalm 50:7-15): We are grateful for what we have and who we have around us. We are genuinely thankful for what God has given us. Although we are surrounded by a world of entitlement, we must choose the attitude of gratitude. Look for the good in life and it will find you.

IMPROVING YOUR SERVE

My son is into the game of tennis. In our spare time, he and I watch a spirited tennis match. We discovered that several matches are won on account of what is called a power serve. A power serve can climb to the whopping speed of nearly 150 miles per hour, making it close to impossible for the opponent to return the serve.

There are 'power serves' in life. This is where we become excellent in our service to and for others. We meet a need before we are asked to do it. We see a gap and fill it without the need for a committee's approval. A power serve of life is going the extra mile just because it's a part of who you are, it's in your DNA.

The Power Serve begins right now with whom you currently serve alongside. When you are a part of a praise team, you are given the golden opportunity to improve your serve.

We want to be worship teams that celebrate our strengths while covering our weaknesses. Most of the answers to the struggles we face as a team can be found within the team.

The power serve allows us to extract the best solution out of our team members. I always say, "If you can locate a problem, you are a candidate to help solve it." And, "If you bring me a problem, make sure you bring a possible solution with you."

Instead of mastering critiques, let's major in solutions.

"Jump into the deep end to find solutions, and don't stay in the shallow end to find fault."

PRACTICAL GUIDE

Giving God our best begins with:
1. The Right Attitude (Psalm 4:5)
2. The Right Motive (Gen. 4:1-10; 1 John 4:18)
3. The Right Ingredients
    a. What's in your hand – Gifts, Talents, Life's Work
    b. Humility – Broken, Stripped of Self
    c. Honoring – Total Focus on the Recipient of the Gift
4. The Right Results
    a. Consistency
    b. Faithfulness
    c. Confidence
    d. Celebration of Others
    e. Sincerity
    f. Thankfulness

How do I improve my serve?

If you can locate a problem, you are a candidate to help solve it.

If you bring your leader a problem, make sure you bring a possible solution with you.

Jump in the deep end to find solutions, and don't stay in the shallow end to find fault.

REFERENCES

Page 8

"Jesus Is the Answer" – By Andrae Crouch & Sandra Crouch, Copyright (c) 1973 Bud John Songs (ASCAP)

"Oh Happy Day" – By Edwin R. Hawkins, published by Edwin R. Hawkins Music co. c/o EMI U

"I Wish We'd All Been Ready" – By Larry Norman, Copyright Beechwood Music Corp. EMI Music

Page 28

Dr. Carlton R. Arthurs – www.carltonarthursministries.com

Page 32

Pastor James E. Ward, Jr. – www.jamesewardjr.com

Page 33

Terry Savelle-Foy – www.terry.com

Page 65

"Nothing But the Blood of Jesus" – By Robert Lowry (1876)

Page 79

Prayer Altars – By John Mulinde and Mark Daniel, World Trumpet Mission Publishing, 2013

ABOUT THE AUTHOR

As a songwriter, author, and worship pastor, Brannon has devoted his life to fulfilling God's mandate to helping people make a genuine connection with God (Psalm 2:8). For over 25 years his ministry has touched the lives of thousands of people both here and abroad. He has ministered in over 15 nations and continues to spread the gospel in both word and song.

While serving for five years at Oral Roberts University as a worship leader and music ministries director, he has shared the stage with great pioneers of the faith and has experienced world-class camaraderie with international worship leaders. For over 16 years, Brannon directed the worship department as well as served as Worship Pastor at Wheaton Christian Center in Carol Stream, Illinois, under the leadership of founding pastor, the late Dr. Carlton R. Arthurs, and lead pastor, Paul D. Arthurs. More recently, Brannon has accepted the position of Campus Pastor at Insight Church under the leadership of Pastor James E. Ward, Jr.

Brannon and his lovely wife Denise, son Benaiah, and daughter Abigail, currently reside in a suburb of Chicago.

www.ingramcontent.com/pod-product-compliance
Lightning Source LLC
Chambersburg PA
CBHW030050100426
42734CB00038B/993